Soups On!

Vegetarian Soups, Muffins & Accompaniments

Barb Bloomfield

Book Publishing Company
Summertown, Tennessee

Cover Design: Cheryl Karas
Interior Design: Warren C. Jefferson
Back Cover Photo: Valerie Epstein
Illustrations: Otis Maly & Warren C. Jefferson

Published in the United States by Book Publishing Company
PO Box 99
Summertown, TN 38483

ISBN 1-57067-047-1

Bloomfield, Barb, 1950-
     Soups on! : vegetarian soups, muffins & accompaniments / Barb
Bloomfield.
          p.   cm.
     Includes index.
     ISBN 1-57067-047-1 (alk. paper)
     1. Soups. 2. Vegetarian cookery. 3. Muffins. I. Title.
TX757.B55 1997
641.8'13--dc21   97-17644
                                                        CIP

Special Lay-Flat Binding
The binding of this book will make it easier for the book to lay open
as you use it and will increase its life span. By opening the book to
any page and running your finger down the spine, the pages will lay
flat without breaking the spine.

Calculations for the nutritional analyses in this book are based on the
average number of servings listed with the recipes and the average
amount of an ingredient, if a range is called for. Calculations are
rounded up to the nearest gram. If two options for an ingredient are
listed, the first one is used. Not included are optional ingredients,
serving suggestions, or fat used for frying, unless the amount of fat
is specified in the recipe.

Contents

Dedicated

to

Dad,

whose concern for others

and diligent, humorous approach to life

I'll always admire and love,

and to

my husband's dad, Gene,

whose love for his family

and care for humanity

is an inspiration to us all.

Soups

Soups

Making soup is such a satisfying and creative activity, whether you have the time to enjoy cooking or you're in a hurry to feed your family or company.

Soup recipes are usually flexible and will accommodate creative substitutions. This book should be like a guide book for you . . . look at these recipes and make them your own, wherever that takes you. Your common sense will steer you as you improvise or experiment, using these recipes as a reference.

Many of these are large recipes which make for good leftovers, but if they're too much for you, it's easy to divide the recipes in half and procede. Using leftovers from other dinners can also be a handy way to start to a soup. A vegetable stir-fry, hash browned potatoes, chili, spaghetti, rice pilaf, burgers, casserole–whatever! Embelish it and create a soup from what you have around.

Stock

I'm not providing stock recipes because I see making stock as an extra step. My advice for creating good soup stock is SAVE . . . bean cooking liquid, vegetable or tempeh steaming liquid, small amounts of gravy or sauces . . . don't throw out liquids leftover from cooking. Keep a jar of liquid/stock in your refrigerator and use it up every week.

There are various vegetarian stock possibilities available on the market. They come in the form of broth powders, cubes (bouillon), and canned stock. For a complete selection of vegetarian broth powders (vegetable, "beef," "chicken," "ham," and "seafood"), contact The Mail Order Catalog, P.O. Box 180, Summertown, TN 38483, or called them at 1-800-695-2241. Miso (see page 123) always makes a flavorful broth, whether you use the light and mild or the dark and pungent varieties.

Blended Soups

Creamy soups are easy and fun to make. A food processor works as well as a blender. It will usually take several batches of blending, so have a spare mixing bowl on hand in which to put the blended or processed soup. When all the contents of the soup pot from which you're blending is empty, you can pour the contents from the bowl back into the pot, and bring back up to heat.

If you're using a blender to combine hot ingredients, put a clean cloth over the top of the blender, underneath the lid, before you turn the blender on. This keeps the mixture from bursting out from under the lid. No matter what you're blending, be sure to leave several inches of airspace in the blender container before you start.

Soup adjustments

Every time you make a soup there are variables that can give you different results. How juicy are your tomatoes? How large are your onions or potatoes? How fresh are your herbs and spices? How thick is your milk? What size is your measuring cup (I have 2 measuring cups that are ⅛ cup different from each other!)?

Here are some ideas for last minute alterations:

If you make a soup that turns out too thin, try one of these for thickening: watered down mashed potatoes; corn starch or white flour dissolved in a few spoons of water; or cooked grain (rice, rolled oats, barley, kasha, etc.) blended with enough water to make a thick paste. Or add a few tablespoons of uncooked couscous, cover, and let set 10 minutes. The couscous will thicken your soup.

If your soup is too salty or spicey, chop a raw potato and boil it in your soup (this won't work for a creamed base soup). The potato absorbs the salt/spice and can be removed if it doesn't go along with your other soup ingredients.

If your soup is too bland, add more of the herbs or spices that are in the recipe. Herbs added towards the end of cooking are just as flavorful as those cooked down for a while.

Don't count on salt to bring out flavor, count on herbs and spices!

Cold soups

I don't have a section for cold soups because I have a confession to make...I love cold leftovers. I can't think of a soup here that I wouldn't enjoy cold the next day, BUT that's not to say that some soups aren't meant to be eaten cold. Gazpacho, chilled creamy cucumber-dill soup, berry/fruit blends, avocado soup, and so many more all make for a good summer lunch. Creamy soups, especially, lend themselves to be eaten cold.

Cream soups

Let me add a tip here...REMEMBER not to boil soups that use blended tofu or nondairy milk as a base. Boiling will cause the creamy soup to turn into curds and whey or separate, which you'll usually want to avoid.

Meat substitutes

Soups are traditionally made with animal products. Chicken and beef soup stock are classic bases for soup in cuisines around the world over.

Eating flesh is a decision that everyone has to make for themselves, but if you decide to give it up, you'll find there are many alternatives that are not only tasty but good for you. The versatile soybean has provided us with many possibilities: tofu (which now comes: firm, medium, soft, silken, low-fat, no-fat, water-packed, aseptically sealed, dried, etc.), tempeh, and textured vegetable protein. Seitan, made from the protein in wheat, is chewy, high in protein, and a superb addition to soup. And, of course, beans of all sorts (and many there are) always provide variety to vegetable soups.

Tomato-Based Soups

Black Bean, Rice & Squash Soup

Yield: 10 cups

If you have other beans already cooked, they can make an interesting variation.

3 Tbsp chopped garlic (one head)
1 Tbsp olive oil

In a soup pot, sauté the garlic in the oil until soft and brown.

4 cups water
¾ cup brown rice
1 bay leaf

Add the water, rice, and bay leaf to the browned garlic, cover, and bring to a boil. Lower the heat to a simmer, and cook for 25 minutes.

3½ cups puréed tomatoes
3 cups bite-sized pieces butternut squash
1 cup chopped parsley
2 tsp fennel seed
½ tsp dried red pepper (optional)

Add the tomatoes, squash, parsley, and spices to the soup. Return to a low boil, cover, and cook for 15 more minutes.

3 cups cooked black beans
1 tsp salt

Add the beans and salt, and cook gently for 5 more minutes. Turn off the heat and leave covered until ready to serve.

Per 2 cups: Calories: 389, Protein: 13 gm., Fat: 4 gm., Carbohydrates: 75 gm.

Black-Eyed Pea Soup with Eggplant

Yield: 13 cups

This soup is easy to prepare, but an unusual combination of herbs and spices makes it a real treat.

1 onion, chopped (2 cups)
1 green pepper, chopped (1½ cups)
1 eggplant, cubed (5 cups)
2 tsp olive oil

In a large soup pot, sauté the onion, green pepper, and eggplant in the oil until they are soft.

4 cups cooked black-eyed peas
4 cups stock or water
3½ cups puréed tomatoes
1 tsp basil
1 tsp thyme
1 tsp nutmeg
1 tsp salt

Add the black-eyed peas, stock, tomatoes, basil, thyme, nutmeg, and salt, and cook for 15 minutes, stirring several times. Remove from the heat, cover, and let set several minutes before serving for the flavors to blend.

Per 2 cups: Calories: 233, Protein: 9 gm., Fat: 2 gm., Carbohydrates: 44 gm.

Broccoli Mushroom Soup

Yield: 8 cups

1 medium onion, chopped
2 cups chopped mushrooms
1 Tbsp chopped garlic
1 tsp olive oil

In a medium soup pot, sauté the onion, mushrooms, and garlic in the olive oil until soft.

6 cups water

Add the water to the pot, and bring to a boil.

4 cups bite-size pieces broccoli
1 cup textured vegetable protein
1 tsp oregano
1 tsp basil
1 tsp rosemary

Add the broccoli, textured vegetable protein, oregano, basil, and rosemary to the boiling water, and simmer for 5 minutes.

1 tsp salt
4 Tbsp tomato paste

Add the salt and tomato paste, and cook for 5 more minutes. Serve immediately.

Per 2 cups: Calories: 136, Protein: 13 gm., Fat: 0 gm., Carbohydrates: 17 gm.

Cabbage Barley Soup

Yield: 14 cups

6 cups stock or water
1 cup barley
1 bay leaf

In a large soup pot, bring the stock, barley, and bay leaf to a boil, and cook for 15 minutes.

8 oz tempeh, cut into small cubes
1 Tbsp canola oil
1 Tbsp soy sauce

In a medium skillet, brown the tempeh in the oil, stirring continuously to keep from sticking. Sprinkle the soy sauce over the tempeh while it cooks. Set aside to add to the soup at the end.

2 Tbsp minced garlic
2 cups cubed butternut squash
4 cups chopped cabbage
2 cups chopped celery
1 green pepper, chopped

Add the garlic, squash, cabbage, celery, and green pepper to the soup pot, and simmer for 20-25 minutes

3 cups puréed tomatoes
½ cup fresh squeezed lemon juice

Add the tomatoes, lemon juice, and browned tempeh. Bring to a boil, turn off the heat, cover, and let set for several minutes before serving.

Per 2 cups: Calories: 225, Protein: 9 gm., Fat: 4 gm., Carbohydrates: 37 gm.

Colorful Curry Soup

Yield: 14 cups

¼ cup chopped garlic
1 tsp black mustard seeds
1 tsp canola oil

In a large soup pot, sauté the garlic and mustard seeds in the oil, stirring constantly, until the seeds pop.

6 cups stock
1½ cups chopped red peppers
1½ cups chopped carrots
2 cups cubed potatoes, cut into ½-inch squares

Add the stock, red peppers, carrots, and potatoes, and bring to a boil. Reduce the heat, cover, and simmer for 15 minutes.

⅓ cup grated gingerroot
2 tsp coriander
1 Tbsp paprika
2 Tbsp curry powder
⅛ tsp cayenne pepper, or to taste
1 tsp salt
1¼ cups tomato sauce
1¼ cups tomato juice
1 cup lemon juice
2 cups frozen or fresh peas
3 cups cooked chick-peas
2 cups (4 oz) mung bean sprouts

Add the spices, tomato sauce and juice, lemon juice, peas, chick-peas, and mung bean sprouts. Return to a boil, lower the heat, and simmer for 10 minutes.

1 cup coconut milk

Turn off the heat, stir in the coconut milk, cover, and keep warm until ready to serve.

Per 2 cups: Calories: 340, Protein: 10 gm., Fat: 8 gm., Carbohydrates: 53 gm.

Eggplant Caponata Soup

Yield: 8 cups

Caponata is traditionally a Mediterranean hors d'oeuvre. This variation makes a delicious soup for those who enjoy the piquant flavors.

1 large onion, chopped
6 cups peeled, finely cubed eggplant
1½ cups chopped celery
1 Tbsp chopped garlic
1 Tbsp olive oil

In a soup pot, sauté the onion, eggplant, celery, and garlic in the oil until all the vegetables are soft.

2 cups water
4 cups crushed tomatoes
½ cup chopped stuffed green olives

Add the water, tomatoes, and olives to the soup, and simmer for 10 minutes.

2 Tbsp balsamic vinegar
2 Tbsp lemon juice

Add the vinegar and lemon juice, stir well, and turn off the heat.

Per 2 cups: Calories: 221, Protein: 4 gm., Fat: 6 gm., Carbohydrates: 38 gm.

Eggplant-Spaghetti Soup

Yield: 10 cups

This soup has a blend of vegetables in addition to pieces of spaghetti. It's a good accompaniment to salad and Bread Sticks (page 114).

2 cups chopped celery
1 large onion, chopped
8 cloves garlic, minced
5 cups peeled, cubed eggplant
** (1 medium)**
2 tsp olive oil

In a soup pot, sauté the celery, onion, garlic, and eggplant in the oil over medium heat. Stir often and cover the pot until the vegetables are soft.

6 cups hot water
1 (28-oz) can crushed tomatoes
1 Tbsp crushed basil
2 tsp oregano
1 tsp salt

Add the water, tomatoes, and spices to the soup, and bring to a boil.

1 cup vermicelli, broken into 1-inch
pieces, or other small pasta

Add the pasta to the boiling soup, and cook for 10 minutes. Turn off the heat, cover, and let set for 10 minutes before serving.

Nutritional yeast (optional)

Garnish with nutritional yeast, if desired.

Per 2 cups: Calories: 237, Protein: 6 gm., Fat: 2 gm., Carbohydrates: 47 gm.

Lentil Soup Deluxe

Yield: 12 cups

8 cups water
1 bay leaf
2 cups lentils
2 Tbsp chopped or pressed garlic
3 cups chopped zucchini

In a large pot, bring the water to a boil with the bay leaf, lentils, garlic, and zucchini. Partially cover and simmer for 30 minutes.

3½ cups finely chopped cabbage
  (¼ large head)
1½ cups chopped carrots
  (3 carrots)
1 (28-oz) can crushed tomatoes
⅓ cup chopped fresh parsley
1 tsp paprika
1 tsp savory
1 tsp dried basil

Add the cabbage, carrots, tomatoes, parsley, and herbs to the soup. Return to a boil and simmer for 20 minutes.

1 tsp salt

Add the salt and keep the soup covered until ready to serve.

Per 2 cups: Calories: 268, Protein: 15 gm., Fat: 0 gm., Carbohydrates: 50 gm.

Mexican Soup-Stew

Yield: 11 cups

A thick and spicy soup to warm you more ways than one.

8 cups water
5 cups chopped green beans, in
   1-inch pieces
½ cup quinoa

In a soup pot, bring the water to a boil, and add the green beans and quinoa. Cover and simmer for 10 minutes.

1 large onion, chopped
2 Tbsp minced garlic
½ Tbsp olive oil
2 Tbsp soy sauce

In a medium skillet, sauté the onion and garlic in the olive oil and soy sauce until soft.

1 cup textured vegetable protein
   (flakes or small chunks are best)

Add the textured vegetable protein to the onion and garlic, and stir until brown.

2 cups corn
4 Tbsp tomato paste
½ cup chopped cilantro
1 Tbsp chili powder
1 Tbsp cumin
½ tsp crushed hot pepper flakes
½ tsp salt

Add the corn, tomato paste, and spices to the soup pot. Add the browned onions and textured vegetable protein, and stir well. Simmer for 10 minutes. Turn off the heat, cover, and let set for 10 minutes before serving.

Per 2 cups: Calories: 301, Protein: 16 gm., Fat: 3 gm., Carbohydrates: 51 gm.

Middle Eastern Lentil Soup

Yield: 11 cups

2 cups lentils
6 cups water

Cook the lentils in the water for 15 minutes.

3 cups cubed potatoes, chopped in ½-inch squares

Add the potatoes to the cooking lentils. Return to a low boil, and cook for 20 minutes.

1 large onion, chopped
2 tsp olive oil

In a medium skillet, sauté the onion in the oil until it is soft and beginning to brown.

1 (28-oz) can crushed tomatoes
½ tsp crushed hot pepper flakes
1 tsp cumin
1 tsp allspice
1 tsp coriander
1 tsp salt

Add the tomatoes, spices, and sautéed onions to the soup. Continue to cook at a low boil for 15 minutes. Test to make sure the lentils are soft. If they are soft, turn off the heat, cover, and let set for 15 minutes. If the lentils are still crunchy, simmer until they are soft. Stir frequently to prevent the soup from sticking to the bottom of the pot.

Juice of 1 lemon

Remove the soup from the heat, add the lemon juice, and stir well.

Per 2 cups: Calories: 322, Protein: 14 gm., Fat: 2 gm., Carbohydrates: 61 gm.

Minestrone

Yield: 9 cups

My high school home-economics class created this recipe. They nixed the traditional combination of zucchini, corn, and peas, but feel free to use your available choice of vegetables. The Salsa-Corn Muffins (page 106) are good with this soup.

5 cups water
1 stalk celery, chopped
1 onion, chopped
1 medium green pepper, chopped
2 cups finely chopped cabbage
2 carrots, chopped
2 medium potatoes, chopped
1 tsp garlic powder
1 tsp basil
1 tsp oregano
½ cup chopped fresh parsley

In a large pot, bring the water, celery, onion, green pepper, cabbage, carrots, potatoes, garlic, basil, oregano, and parsley to a boil. Simmer for 15 minutes.

2 cups cooked macaroni (If you don't have this already cooked, add it with the first batch of ingredients after the soup has been cooking for 5 minutes.)
1½ cups cooked pinto or navy beans
1 (15-oz) can tomato sauce

Add the noodles, beans, and tomato sauce to the soup, and cook for 5 more minutes.

Turn off the heat and serve. This is good with nutritional yeast as a garnish.

Per 2 cups: Calories: 277, Protein: 9 gm., Fat: 0 gm., Carbohydrates: 57 gm.

Red, White & Green Bean Soup

Yield: 12 cups

This is a colorful soup—fun for both kids and adults to eat. If you don't have fresh green beans, use canned ones, but add them with the last group of ingredients.

1 large onion, chopped (1½ cups)
1 lb tofu, cut in ½-inch cubes
8 oz fresh mushrooms, chopped
2 tsp olive oil
1 Tbsp soy sauce

In a large soup pot, sauté the onion, tofu, and mushrooms in the olive oil and soy sauce. Stir several times until the onions and tofu are browned.

6 cups boiling water
4 cups fresh chopped green beans, in 1-inch pieces

Add the boiling water and green beans to the soup pot, and cook for 5 minutes.

1 cup uncooked elbow macaroni

Add the macaroni to the soup pot, and cook for 10 more minutes.

1 (14.5-oz) can diced tomatoes and green chilies
1 (15-oz) can tomato sauce
1 cup chopped fresh parsley
1 Tbsp paprika
½ tsp salt

Simmer for 5 more minutes, and serve.

Per 2 cups: Calories: 221, Protein: 11 gm., Fat: 5 gm., Carbohydrates: 32 gm.

Seitan Soup with Cabbage

Yield: 14 cups

This is a very filling soup with chewy pieces of seitan amidst the tasty vegetables.

1¼ cups instant gluten flour (vital wheat gluten)
½ tsp garlic powder or granules
3 Tbsp nutritional yeast
⅞ cup water

In a medium mixing bowl, mix the gluten flour with the garlic, nutritional yeast, and ⅞ cup water. This will make a stiff dough which you can work with your hands. It is not necessary to knead the dough; just shape it into a 2- to 3-inch log. Then slice it into 8-9 half-inch pieces.

3 Tbsp soy sauce
4 cups water

Bring the soy sauce and water to a boil in a medium saucepan.

Stretch out the pieces of dough before slipping them into the boiling water/soy sauce mixture. Reduce to a simmer and cook for 20 minutes.

2 cups chopped celery
2 cups chopped onion
2 Tbsp minced garlic
1 Tbsp canola oil

In a large soup pot, sauté the celery, onion, and garlic in the oil until soft. Stir to prevent sticking.

4 cups chopped cabbage
3 cups cubed potatoes

3½ cups puréed tomatoes
3 Tbsp paprika
1 tsp thyme
1½ tsp caraway seeds
¼ cup chopped fresh parsley
1 Tbsp liquid sweetener
1 tsp salt

Add the stock from the cooked seitan to the soup pot, then add the cabbage and potatoes. Bring to a boil and cook gently for 25 minutes. While the soup is cooking, chop the cooked seitan patties into ½-inch cubes. Set aside to add with the next batch of ingredients.

Add the seitan, tomatoes, and seasonings to the soup, and simmer another 5 minutes.

Per 2 cups: Calories: 268, Protein: 25 gm., Fat: 2 gm., Carbohydrates: 35 gm.

Turnip Chowder

Yield: 8½ cups

A creamy tomato soup base with turnips as a predominant flavor makes this soup a special treat.

3 cups water
1 cup cubed carrots
2½ cups cubed turnips, cut in ½-inch squares (3 medium turnips)
1 onion, chopped
1 bay leaf

Bring the water, carrots, turnips, onion, and bay leaf to a boil, lower the heat, and simmer for 20 minutes.

3 Tbsp tomato paste
2½ cups cooked lima beans
1 cup nondairy milk
½ tsp salt
3 Tbsp nutritional yeast

Dissolve the tomato paste in a little hot soup broth, then stir back into the soup. Add the lima beans, nondairy milk, salt, and nutritional yeast to the simmered vegetables. Bring the soup up slowly to just below a boil, and simmer a few minutes. Turn off the heat and serve.

Per 2 cups: Calories: 227, Protein: 12 gm., Fat: 1 gm., Carbohydrates: 41 gm.

Miso-Based Soups

End-of-the-Season Garden Soup

Yield: 12 cups

Before that last frost, we bring in the last of the basil, peppers, and cherry tomatoes, dig the carrots, and plant fall greens. This soup came about from a basket of produce picked at that time.

1½ cups chopped bell peppers
2 cups chopped onion
2 cups chopped mushrooms
2 tsp olive oil

In a soup pot, sauté the peppers, onion, and mushrooms in the oil until soft.

8 cups water
4 cups sliced carrots
½ cup millet

Add the water, carrots, and millet to the pot, bring to a boil, and cook for 10 minutes.

1 cup fresh parsley
½ cup fresh basil

Finely chop the fresh herbs, and add to soup.

2 cups whole cherry tomatoes
1 tsp garlic powder
¼ cup soy sauce

Add the cherry tomatoes, garlic powder, and soy sauce. Bring to a boil, then turn off the heat.

2 Tbsp miso

Dissolve the miso in ½ cup of liquid from the soup pot. Add the miso to the soup pot after the heat has been turned off. Cover until you're ready to serve.

If you need to reheat this soup, remember not to boil it, or the enzymes in the miso will be destroyed.

Per 2 cups: Calories: 183, Protein: 6 gm., Fat: 2 gm., Carbohydrates: 32 gm.

Garden Soup

Yield: 11 cups

This is a thick soup that is chock full of goodness, especially if you use fresh organic vegetables. Use a food processor to chop the vegetables if you're in a hurry.

1 large bell pepper, chopped
1 large onion, chopped
2 cups diced carrots
2 small jalapeño peppers, minced
(optional)
1 Tbsp olive oil

Sauté the vegetables for 10 minutes in the olive oil, stirring several times.

4 cups tomatoes
1 cup fresh herbs: basil, parsley,
chives, marjoram, oregano, etc.

Chop the tomatoes and herbs in a food processor. Add to the soup pot, and cook for 15 more minutes.

2 cups cooked rice
2 cups cooked corn

Add the cooked rice and corn, bring to a boil, and turn off the heat.

4 Tbsp dark miso
1 cup warm water

Dissolve the miso in the warm water, and stir into the soup after the heat has been turned off. Cover the soup if not serving immediately.

If you need to reheat this soup, remember not to boil it, or the enzymes in the miso will be destroyed.

Per 2 cups: Calories: 245, Protein: 6 gm., Fat: 4 gm., Carbohydrates: 46 gm.

Kraut Soup

Yield: 11 cups

If you like the salty-sour flavor of sauerkraut, this soup is for you.

1 cup chopped green onions
1 tsp olive oil

In a large soup pot, sauté the green onions in the oil until soft.

4 cups water
3-4 cups chopped zucchini
1½ cups chopped carrots

Add the water, zucchini, and carrots. Bring to a boil, reduce the heat, and simmer for 15 minutes.

2 cups cooked navy beans
1½ cups sauerkraut
1 tsp thyme
2 tsp paprika

Add the beans, sauerkraut, thyme, and paprika to the soup. Return to a boil for several minutes while you stir it well. Turn off the heat.

2½ Tbsp light miso

Add the miso and mix it well with the soup broth.

If you need to reheat this soup, remember not to boil it, or the enzymes in the miso will be destroyed.

Per 2 cups: Calories: 162, Protein: 7 gm., Fat: 2 gm., Carbohydrates: 29 gm.

Miso Escarole Soup

Yield: 12 cups

The curly leaves of escarole top off a tossed salad with flair, but try them also in soup. Mild yet distinctive, they add color and texture to this thick, miso-based soup.

1 onion, chopped
1 lb tofu, cubed
1 Tbsp soy sauce
2 tsp olive oil

In a large soup pot, sauté the onion and tofu in the soy sauce and olive oil until browned.

7 cups water
1 bay leaf
1 Tbsp garlic powder or granules
1¼ cups chopped butternut squash or carrots
3 medium potatoes, chopped
⅓ cup millet

Add the water, bay leaf, garlic, squash or carrots, potatoes, and millet to the soup pot. Bring to a boil and cook for 10 minutes.

1 large head escarole, chopped (6 cups)

Add the escarole and cook 5 more minutes. Turn off the heat.

¼ cup red (white rice) miso
½ cup warm water
2 Tbsp toasted sesame seeds, for garnish (optional)

Dissolve the miso in the warm water, and add to the the soup. Cover and let set for several minutes before serving. Sprinkle the sesame seeds over each bowl as it is served, if desired. This soup thickens as it sets. If you have any leftover, you may need to add more water when reheating.

If you need to reheat this soup, remember not to boil it, or the enzymes in the miso will be destroyed.

Per 2 cups: Calories: 263, Protein: 11 gm., Fat: 6 gm., Carbohydrates: 40 gm.

Mushroom Vegetable Barley Soup

Yield: 13 cups

3 cups water
1 cup pearled barley
1 bay leaf

In a small saucepan, bring the water, barley, and bay leaf to a boil. Simmer for 15 minutes.

1 tsp olive oil
1 onion, chopped (1½ cups)
1½ cups chopped mushrooms
1 cup chopped celery (with tops)
3 parsnips, chopped
2 carrots, chopped
1½ cups chopped zucchini

Heat the oil in the bottom of a soup pot. Add the onion, mushrooms, celery, parsnips, carrots, and zucchini. Sauté with the lid on, stirring occasionally.

5 cups water
1 tsp thyme
1 tsp basil

Add the water, herbs, and cooked barley to the soup pot, bring to a boil, reduce the heat, and simmer for 5 minutes. Turn off the heat.

¼ cup dark miso
1 cup warm water

Dilute the miso in the warm water, and add it to the soup. Remove the bay leaf and serve immediately.

If you need to reheat this soup, remember not to boil it, or the enzymes in the miso will be destroyed.

Per 2 cups: Calories: 186, Protein: 5 gm., Fat: 2 gm., Carbohydrates: 38 gm.

Napa Cabbage Miso Soup

Yield: 15 cups

The sweet flavor of napa cabbage blends with sweet potato and miso to produce this delicious, easy-to-make soup. While it's cooking, you have time to bake some Scones (page 121) for a complete lunch or supper.

8 cups stock or water
2 cups chopped celery
2 cups chopped green onions
1⅔ Tbsp minced garlic
2 large sweet potatoes, chopped
   (4 cups)
1 large napa cabbage, chopped
   (8 cups)

In a large soup pot, bring the stock to a boil along with the celery, green onions, garlic, sweet potato, and napa cabbage. Cook for 30 minutes, then turn off the heat.

½ cup red (white rice) miso
1 cup warm water
2 tsp toasted sesame oil
Nutritional yeast, for garnish
   (optional)

Dissolve the miso in the warm water, and add to the soup. Add the toasted sesame oil, and stir well. Serve with nutritional yeast to sprinkle on top of each bowl, if desired.

If you need to reheat this soup, remember not to boil it, or the enzymes in the miso will be destroyed.

Per 2 cups: Calories: 153, Protein: 3 gm., Fat: 2 gm., Carbohydrates: 30 gm.

Red Pepper Soup

Yield: 10 cups

The sweetness of red peppers is a treat. This soup is quick and easy to prepare.

1 cup scallions
3 cups chopped red peppers
3 cloves garlic, minced
1 cup textured vegetable protein flakes
2 tsp olive oil

In a soup pot, sauté the scallions, red peppers, garlic, and textured vegetable protein in the oil until they have browned.

7½ cups stock or water
1 cup chopped parsley
2 Tbsp dried dill weed
2 cups cooked rice

Add the stock, parsley, dill weed, and rice to the soup. Bring to a boil, reduce the heat, and simmer for 10 minutes.

6 Tbsp light barley miso
½ cup warm water

Dissolve the miso in the warm water. Remove the soup from the heat, add the miso mixture, and stir.

If you need to reheat this soup, remember not to boil it, or the enzymes in the miso will be destroyed.

Per 2 cups: Calories: 220, Protein: 11 gm., Fat: 3 gm., Carbohydrates: 36 gm.

Rutabaga & Mushroom Soup

Yield: 14 cups

The earthy, comforting taste of rutabagas is one that I enjoy, especially in cold weather. Barley makes a chewy, wholesome contribution. This recipe makes enough soup to last through several meals, unless you have a gang to feed.

7 cups water
½ cup pearled barley
1 large rutabaga, cubed (4 cups)

Bring the water to a boil in a soup pot, and add the barley and rutabaga. Lower the heat and simmer for 20 minutes.

2 cups chopped scallions
2 cups chopped mushrooms
1½ cups cubed tofu, cut in
  ¼ squares
3 cloves garlic, minced

Add the scallions, mushrooms, tofu, and garlic to the soup, and cook for 10 more minutes.

¼ cup dark miso
1 cup hot water

Dissolve the miso in the cup of hot water, and add it to the soup. Remove from the heat and serve.

If you need to reheat this soup, remember not to boil it, or the enzymes in the miso will be destroyed.

Per 2 cups: Calories: 133, Protein: 7 gm., Fat: 2 gm., Carbohydrates: 19 gm.

Wonton Soup

Yield: 14 cups

5-6 cups finely chopped, packed kale

Steam the kale until tender, about 5-10 minutes.

2 cups chopped onion
1 tsp olive oil
1 cup crumbled firm tofu
1 Tbsp soy sauce

In a medium skillet, sauté the onion in the oil until it starts to brown. Add the tofu and soy sauce to the skillet, and cook until all the moisture has evaporated. Drain the steamed kale and add it to the skillet.

8 cups water
1 cup chopped celery
2 cups chopped carrots
1 tsp garlic powder
4 vegetable bouillon cubes

In a large soup pot, bring the 8 cups water to a boil along with the celery, carrots, garlic powder, and vegetable cubes. Simmer for 10 minutes.

1 (12-oz) package wonton wrappers

While the soup is simmering, fill each wonton wrapper with 1 tablespoon of the tofu/kale filling. Fold the opposite corners of the wrapper into the middle, and seal with a dot of water. Set aside on a cookie sheet until it is time to drop into the soup.

⅓ cup miso
½ cup warm water

Dissolve the miso in the ½ cup warm water.

Per 2 cups: Calories: 264, Protein: 10 gm., Fat: 3 gm., Carbohydrates: 47 gm.

Drop the wontons gently into the simmering soup, and let them set while the soup returns to a boil. Don't stir the soup or the wontons will break apart. You may need to spoon some of the liquid up over the wontons to cover them with broth. Simmer for 2 minutes. Turn off the heat and add the dissolved miso. Stir gently and serve immediately.

If you need to reheat this soup, remember not to boil it, or the enzymes in the miso will be destroyed.

Zucchini Soup

Yield: 10 cups

To keep fresh shiitake mushrooms from getting tough when you cook them, remember to use low heat. This soup is delicately flavored by the red miso (white rice miso) as well as the shiitakes and scallions.

1 tsp olive oil
3 cups fresh shiitake mushrooms, stems removed, chopped into small cubes
1 Tbsp soy sauce

In a medium skillet, sauté the mushrooms in the oil and soy sauce over low heat. Cover and cook for 15 minutes, stirring occasionally. After 15 minutes, turn off the heat, leaving the lid on until ready to add them to the soup pot. While these are cooking, prepare the rest of the soup.

¼ cup millet

In a flat-bottomed soup pot, dry-roast the millet until it pops and turns light brown.

6 cups boiling water
4 cups chopped zucchini
2 cups chopped scallions (two bunches—use both the green and white parts)
1 cup chopped carrots

Add the boiling water, zucchini, scallions, and carrots to the toasted millet. Return to a boil and cook for 15 minutes.

Per 2 cups: Calories: 192, Protein: 7 gm., Fat: 2 gm., Carbohydrates: 34 gm.

6 Tbsp red (white rice) miso
¼ cup warm water

Dissolve the miso in warm water. If you don't have red miso, you can use a darker or lighter miso. Use less dark miso because its flavor is stronger.

After the soup has cooked for 15 minutes, turn the heat to very low, and add the shiitakes and dissolved miso. Stir and heat through until hot enough to eat. Keep covered until ready to serve.

If you need to reheat this soup, remember not to boil it, or the enzymes in the miso will be destroyed.

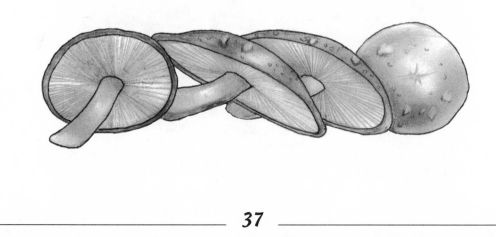

Puréed & Creamy Soups

Asparagus Soup

Yield: 10 cups

Be sure to use fresh asparagus so you can enjoy its subtle flavor.

6 cups stock or water
2 lbs asparagus, chopped (Set the tips aside to add later.)
3 cups chopped potatoes
1½ cups chopped celery
1 large onion, chopped

Place the stock or water, chopped asparagus, potatoes, celery, and onion in a soup pot, bring to a boil, and simmer until everything is soft, about 10 minutes. Blend in a food processor in several small batches.

The asparagus tips
1 tsp dried basil
1 tsp salt
⅛ tsp black pepper

Add the asparagus tips, basil, salt, and black pepper to the blended soup. Simmer for 5 minutes.

1¾ cups nondairy milk

Add the milk to the soup, stir well, and turn off the heat. If you let the soup boil with the milk in it, it may separate into curds and whey.

Per 2 cups: Calories: 171, Protein: 7 gm., Fat: 1 gm., Carbohydrates: 32 gm.

Butternut Soup

Yield 8 cups

My friend Willa told me about this delicious soup. It was served at a cafe she worked at in Berkeley. It is a creamy orange soup with dark basil flecks—so easy and so good.

7 cups peeled and cubed raw butternut squash*
1 Tbsp chopped garlic
5 cups water

In a medium soup pot, boil the butternut squash and garlic in the water for 15 minutes. Blend in a food processor or blender in several batches until smooth. Pour the blended mixture back into the pot, and bring to a simmer just below boiling.

1 Tbsp finely crushed dried basil
½ tsp salt

Add the basil and salt, and continue to simmer for 5 minutes, stirring occasionally. Serve right away or cover until ready to serve.

*Butternut squash is easy to peel with a good potato peeler. Just the outer skin needs to be removed. It's alright to leave the light green layer you will find between the skin and the orange fruit on a fresh squash.

Per 2 cups: Calories: 141, Protein: 3 gm., Fat: 0 gm., Carbohydrates: 34 gm.

Carrot Tarragon Soup

Yield: 6 cups

Try this simple soup with the flavor of tarragon and the color of carrots.

4½ cups water
4 cups chopped carrots
2 cloves garlic, chopped
½ cup chopped fresh tarragon

Bring the water, carrots, garlic, and tarragon to a boil, and simmer for 10 minutes.

Place the contents in a food processor or blender in several batches, and blend until smooth, and return to the soup pot.

1 Tbsp balsamic vinegar
½ tsp salt

Add the vinegar and salt to the soup. Bring to a boil, stirring to prevent sticking; then turn off the heat and serve.

Per 1 cup: Calories: 49, Protein: 1 gm., Fat: 0 gm., Carbohydrates: 11 gm.

Corn Chowder

Yield: 11 cups

This soup is creamy and tasty and one you'll want to make again and again. Homemade Crackers (page 115) are good with this soup.

5 cups chopped potatoes
4 cups water

In a soup pot, cook the potatoes in the water for 5-10 minutes until they are soft. Then blend them in your food processor or blender, and pour the creamy liquid back into the soup pot.

1 bell pepper, chopped
1 onion, chopped
1 tsp olive oil

In a skillet, sauté the bell pepper and onion in the oil until they are soft and start to brown. Add them to the creamy potato soup base. If you're using frozen or fresh corn, add it to the skillet of sautéed vegetables, and cook the corn briefly before adding it to the blended potato soup base.

4 cups corn (frozen, fresh, or canned)
2 cups nondairy milk
½ cup chopped fresh parsley
1 tsp salt
⅛ tsp black pepper

Add the corn (if you didn't add it to the sautéed vegetables), nondairy milk, parsley, salt, and black pepper to the soup pot. Gradually return the soup to a slow boil, stirring often so it won't stick to the bottom of the pot. Simmer for several minutes. Don't sustain a rolling boil, or the milk may separate. Remove from the heat and cover until ready to serve.

Per 2 cups: Calories: 272, Protein: 6 gm., Fat: 2 gm., Carbohydrates: 56 gm.

Cream of Leek with Fennel Soup

Yield: 9 cups

A light green, creamy soup with flecks of leek strips and a delightfully subtle flavor.

4 cups peeled, cubed potatoes
1 bulb fennel, chopped (2 cups of
   stalk and feathery leaves)
5 cups water

Bring the potatoes and fennel to a boil in the water. Reduce the heat and simmer for 15 minutes.

2 large leeks, chopped into slivers
   (4½ cups of the white and green)
1 Tbsp olive oil

Split the full length of the leeks in half to enable you to wash between each leaf. Chop the leeks, then sauté while stirring in a skillet in the olive oil until the leeks are soft, stirring constantly.

Blend the potato/fennel mixture in a blender or food processor in several batches. Pour the blended mixture back into the soup pot, then add the sautéed leeks.

1 cup nondairy milk
1 tsp salt
Nutritional yeast for garnish

Add the nondairy milk and salt, bring to a high simmer, then turn off the heat. Garnish with nutritional yeast.

Per 2 cups: Calories: 235, Protein: 4 gm., Fat: 4 gm., Carbohydrates: 45 gm.

Creamy Mushroom Soup Deluxe

Yield: 10 cups

4 cups chopped potatoes
4 cups water

Bring the potatoes and water to a boil, and simmer for 10 minutes until soft. Then blend them until smooth in several batches in a blender, and set aside to add to the soup later.

2 Tbsp chopped garlic
1 cup chopped green onions
1½ cups chopped celery
8 oz fresh mushrooms, chopped
1 tsp olive oil

In the bottom of a soup pot, sauté the garlic, green onions, celery, and mushrooms in the oil. Cook until the onions begin to brown and the mushrooms are soft. Stir to prevent sticking.

2 cups nondairy milk
1 Tbsp white flour
½ tsp salt
⅛-¼ tsp black pepper

Add the nondairy milk, flour, salt, and black pepper to the sautéed vegetables. Stir vigorously to dissolve the flour into the milk. Add the blended potatoes and bring to a simmer. Cook for 2 minutes just below boiling so the milk will not separate. Turn off the heat, cover, and let set for several minutes before serving.

Per 2 cups: Calories: 180, Protein: 5 gm., Fat: 2 gm., Carbohydrates: 34 gm.

Easy Cream of Broccoli Soup

Yield: 8-10 cups

This soup is so satisfying and quick to make. We like to eat garlic toast with it.

4 cups chopped broccoli (flowers, stalks, and upper stems)
4 cups cubed potatoes
1 medium onion, chopped
3 cups water

In a soup pot, boil the broccoli, potatoes, and onion in the water for 10 minutes.

1 cup chopped parsley
½ cup chopped fresh dill

Add the parsley and dill to the boiling vegetables, and simmer for 5 more minutes.

3 cups nondairy milk

In a blender or food processor, blend the contents of the soup pot along with the nondairy milk in small batches. Do not overfill the blender or food processor. Put the blended soup back on the stove, and heat slowly but do not boil.

1 tsp salt, or to taste

Add the salt and serve hot.

Per 2 cups: Calories: 212, Protein: 7 gm., Fat: 3 gm., Carbohydrates: 38 gm.

Orange Beet Soup

Yield: 5½ cups

Here is a colorful creamed soup with distinct flavor that is good served hot or cold. This soup makes a good accompaniment to other parts of a meal—a green salad with Onion-Pepper-Rice Muffins (page 102) and a tofu spread is a good combination.

1½ tsp coarsely chopped garlic
4 whole cloves
2 cups beet juice or water
4 cups peeled, chopped beets

Boil the garlic, cloves, beet juice, and beets for 10-15 minutes until the beets are soft. Blend these ingredients in a food processor or blender. Be careful not to overfill your blender jar, or you'll be cleaning up beet juice!

1½ cups orange juice (fresh squeezed is best)
½ tsp salt (optional)

Add the orange juice and stir well. Heat up if serving hot, or cool down if serving cold.

Per 1 cup: Calories: 68, Protein: 1 gm., Fat: 0 gm., Carbohydrates: 15 gm.

Spicy Roots Soup

Yield: 10 cups

This is a winter soup which warms you through and through. Serve it with Potato Buns (page 120).

1 large onion, chopped
2 tsp olive oil

In a soup pot, brown the onion in the olive oil while stirring occasionally to keep the onion from sticking.

1 large rutabaga, cubed (3½ cups)
1 large sweet potato, cubed (2 cups)
3 medium beets, cubed (3½ cups)
5 cups water

Add the rutabaga, sweet potato, beets, and water to the soup pot, and boil for 15 minutes.

3 tsp ground ginger
1 tsp cinnamon
1 tsp dry mustard
2 tsp ground cumin
⅛-¼ tsp black pepper

Add the spices to the soup, and cook 5 more minutes. In a food processor, blend 6-8 cups of the soup into a purée. This leaves some of the vegetables in their chunky state. Add the puréed portion back to the soup pot, and return to a low boil. Turn off the heat.

1 tsp salt
1 cup nondairy milk

Add the salt and nondairy milk to the soup, and stir well. Cover the soup and let it set for several minutes before serving. If reheating is needed, do not boil; just simmer.

Per 2 cups: Calories: 156, Protein: 3 gm., Fat: 3 gm., Carbohydrates: 29 gm.

Triple Onion Soup

Yield 10 cups

During the preparation of this soup, my tear ducts worked overtime. It was well worth it, however, for this creamy soup is full of flavor.

4 cups chopped leeks

Remember to slit the leeks up the center so you can wash in between the upper leaves. You can chop up to where the green part gets tough.

1 Tbsp soy margarine
4 cups chopped onion
3 Tbsp chopped garlic

Sauté for 10 minutes, stirring constantly until the vegetables are soft. Remove ¾ cup of the sautéed vegetables to add back later.

6 cups water
1 tsp thyme
½ tsp celery seed

Add the water and spices, and bring to a boil. Cook for 10 minutes at a low boil.

1 (12.3-oz) package firm silken tofu

Blend the tofu along with the contents of the soup pot. Do this in several batches so the soup won't overflow the blender jar. Return the puréed soup to the pot.

½ cup nutritional yeast
2 Tbsp soy sauce
1 tsp salt

Add the nutritional yeast, soy sauce, salt, and the reserved sautéed vegetables to the creamy soup. Mix well and bring just up to a boil, then turn the heat off and cover for several minutes before serving.

Per 2 cups: Calories: 195, Protein: 14 gm., Fat: 4 gm., Carbohydrates: 29 gm.

Black-Eyed Peas & Greens Soup

Yield: 14 cups

Serve this wholesome soup with some grainy muffins, and your meal will be complete.

2½ Tbsp chopped garlic
1 large green pepper, chopped
(2 cups)
1 minced jalapeño pepper
1 Tbsp olive oil

In a soup pot, sauté the garlic and peppers in the oil until soft, stirring occasionally.

6 cups chopped greens (any
combination of kale, collards,
Swiss chard, mustard)
6 cups stock or water

Add the greens and stock or water, bring to a boil, lower the heat, and simmer for 20 minutes.

¼ cup miso
1 cup warm water
3 cups cooked black-eyed peas

Dissolve the miso in the warm water, and add along with the black-eyed peas to the cooked vegetables. Heat until almost boiling, and serve.

If you need to reheat this soup, remember not to boil it, or the enzymes in the miso will be destroyed.

Per 2 cups: Calories: 155, Protein: 7 gm., Fat: 3 gm., Carbohydrates: 24 gm.

Coconut-Lemon-Napa Soup

Yield: 16 cups

This soup is an elegant treat.

1 cup chopped green onions
2 cups chopped celery
3 cups chopped mushrooms
6½ cups chopped napa cabbage
2 Tbsp water

Steam the green onions, celery, mushrooms, and cabbage in the water in a large soup pot for 5-8 minutes. Stir several times and keep covered between stirrings.

1 Tbsp grated gingerroot
5 oz water chestnuts, cut into strips
½ cup fresh squeezed lemon juice
  (3 lemons)
1 head garlic, minced (2 Tbsp)
¼ cup soy sauce
8 cups water

Add the ginger, water chestnuts, lemon juice, garlic, soy sauce, and water, and bring to a boil.

8 oz rice sticks or rice noodles
  (Py Mai Fun)

Break up the rice sticks a little as you drop them into the soup so they are easier to stir in. Cook for 3 minutes and lower the heat.

14 oz coconut milk

Add the coconut milk and simmer for several minutes. Remove from the heat and cover until ready to serve.

Per 2 cups: Calories: 247, Protein: 3 gm., Fat: 9 gm., Carbohydrates: 35 gm.

Crowder Pea/Couscous Stew
with Brussels Sprouts

Yield: 16 cups

Crowder peas are a Southern delicacy and are similar to black-eyed peas. They are combined here with rutabagas, brussels sprouts, and miso to produce a superb, hearty flavor for this thick soup.

2 cups chopped onion
1 green pepper, chopped
1 Tbsp olive oil

In a large soup pot, sauté the onion and green pepper in the oil until browned.

4 cups cubed rutabaga
4 cups brussels sprouts, cut into halves
1½ cups diced carrots
8 cups water

Add the rutabagas, brussels sprouts, carrots, and water to the soup pot. Bring to a boil and simmer for 10 minutes.

1 cup whole wheat couscous
1 cup chopped fresh parsley
2 (15.8-oz) cans crowder peas, drained and rinsed
2 cups fresh or frozen corn

Add the couscous, parsley, crowder peas, and corn. Return to a boil for 1 minute, then turn off the heat, and leave covered.

½ cup miso
1 cup warm water

Dissolve the miso in the cup of warm water, and add to the soup. Stir well and leave covered until ready to serve. If you need to reheat this soup, remember not to boil it, or the enzymes in the miso will be destroyed.

Per 2 cups: Calories: 348, Protein: 14 gm., Fat: 3 gm., Carbohydrates: 64 gm.

Curried Tofu & Vegetable Soup

Yield: 13 cups

This curry soup can be as hot as you wish; just adjust the amount of jalapeño pepper that you add. It also calls for an exotic Indian spice called hing, which adds distinctive flavor.

1½ cups chopped onions
2 cups chopped green peppers
2 cups chopped celery
2 cups chopped carrots
4 cups peeled, cubed eggplant
   (1 eggplant)
1 lb tofu, cut into small cubes
1 jalapeño pepper, minced
1 Tbsp canola oil

In a large soup pot, sauté the onions, green peppers, celery, carrots, eggplant, tofu, and jalapeño in 1 tablespoon oil for 15-20 minutes, stirring occasionally.

½ tsp black mustard seeds
½ tsp cumin seeds
½ tsp canola oil
Pinch of hing

In a small skillet, stir the mustard and cumin seeds into the oil until they pop. Add a pinch of hing, cover the skillet to keep the seeds from popping out of the pan, and shake it a few times. Turn off the heat and add these spices to the pot of soup.

6 cups hot water or stock
2 cups cooked rice
1 cup whole cherry tomatoes or
   chopped tomatoes
1 tsp coriander
1 tsp turmeric
1 Tbsp minced fresh gingerroot
1 tsp salt
3 Tbsp lemon juice

Add the hot water, rice, cherry tomatoes, coriander, turmeric, ginger, salt, and lemon juice to the soup. Bring up to a boil, then lower the heat, and simmer for 5 minutes.

Per 2 cups: Calories: 216, Protein: 8 gm., Fat: 6 gm., Carbohydrates: 31 gm.

Eggplant Basil Soup

Yield: 9 cups

A sweet basil soup with a chewy, rich, stew-like consistency.

1 Tbsp olive oil
1 large onion, chopped
1 large bell pepper, chopped
2 Tbsp minced garlic
3 cups peeled, cubed eggplant

Heat the oil in a heavy bottomed soup pot, and sauté the onion, pepper, garlic, and eggplant.

3 cups water or stock
1 cup textured vegetable protein flakes

Add the water and textured vegetable protein, bring to a boil, and simmer for 5 minutes.

1½ cups mashed sweet potatoes
2 cups water or vegetable stock
1 cup fresh basil leaves

In a blender, combine the sweet potatoes, water or stock, and basil until smooth. Pour this mixture into the cooked textured vegetable protein and vegetables. Bring to a simmer and stir to prevent sticking.

1 tsp salt
2 Tbsp lemon juice

Add the salt and lemon juice to the soup, and simmer for 5 more minutes.

Per 2 cups: Calories: 178, Protein: 10 gm., Fat: 2 gm., Carbohydrates: 27 gm.

Garlic Broccoli Ginger Soup

Yield: 9 cups

This simple soup is strong with flavor. Try it with Onion-Pepper-Rice Muffins (page 102).

2 Tbsp grated ginger
1 head of garlic, pressed
1 tsp olive oil

In a medium soup pot, sauté the ginger and garlic in the olive oil while stirring for several minutes.

6 cups water or soup stock
¼ cup quinoa, well rinsed
1 head broccoli, chopped into bite sized pieces
⅓ cup crumbled kombu (sea vegetable)

Add the water, quinoa, broccoli, and kombu to the pot. Scrape the bottom to mix any garlic or ginger into the water. Cover, bring to a boil, then turn down to a simmer for 15 minutes.

½ tsp salt (optional)

Add salt if desired.

Per 2 cups: Calories: 66, Protein: 3 gm., Fat: 2 gm., Carbohydrates: 10 gm.

Garlic Pinto Soup

Yield: 9 cups

This soup goes well with Tomato Herb Muffins (page 109).

4 cloves garlic, minced
1 tsp olive oil

In the bottom of a medium soup pot, sauté the garlic in the oil.

2 cups water
1 cup chopped fresh parsley
2 cups corn (fresh or frozen)

Add the water, parsley, and corn, and simmer for 5 minutes.

4 cups cooked pinto beans and stock
1 cup cooked rice
1½ tsp cumin
½ tsp salt

Add the beans, rice, cumin, and salt, and bring to a boil. Simmer for 5 more minutes, stirring occasionally to prevent the soup from sticking to the bottom of the pot.

Per 2 cups: Calories: 332, Protein: 13 gm., Fat: 1 gm., Carbohydrates: 65 gm.

Herbed Parsnip-Quinoa Stew

Yield: 15 cups

This stew makes a full pot, and it thickens as it cools. It freezes well so if you have leftovers, freeze some for when you don't have time to cook.

4 stalks celery, chopped (2 cups)
2 onions, chopped (3 cups)
2 tsp olive oil

In a large soup pot, sauté the celery and onion in the olive oil. Stir frequently, covering the pot in between so the vegetables will cook more quickly. Cook until the celery and onion are soft.

1 cup quinoa

Rinse the quinoa for several minutes in a strainer while mixing with your fingers.

4 cups water
3 cups chopped parsnips
6 cups chopped cabbage
4 cups tomato purée
1 tsp crushed rosemary
1½ tsp sage

Add the water, parsnips, cabbage, tomato purée, quinoa, rosemary, and sage to the sautéed vegetables. Bring to a boil and cook for 20 minutes.

5 cups cooked black-eyed peas
1 tsp salt

Add the black-eyed peas and salt to the soup, and return to a boil. Turn off the heat and keep covered until ready to serve.

Per 2 cups: Calories: 462, Protein: 18 gm., Fat: 5 gm., Carbohydrates: 86 gm.

Kasha Leek Stew

Yield: 11 cups

The hearty flavor of roasted kasha is a taste that's unique unto itself. Add some flavorful vegetables and tempeh, and you have a dish your dinner guests will want seconds of.

1 cup kasha

In a large soup pot, dry roast the kasha, stirring constantly.

6 cups boiling water

When the kasha starts to get darker, add the water. It will bubble and steam up, so be careful; don't burn yourself.

2 leeks, chopped into cross-sections (include white and green parts)

Wash the leeks well, opening up the inner leaves so you can remove any dirt.

2 cups chopped turnips
8 oz tempeh, cubed
8 oz mushrooms, chopped
1 bay leaf
1 tsp sage
1 tsp thyme
2 tsp garlic powder

Add the leeks, turnips, tempeh, mushrooms, bay leaf, sage, thyme, and garlic powder to the kasha and water. Bring to a boil, lower the heat, and simmer for 10 minutes.

2 cups frozen peas
1 tsp salt

Stir in the peas and salt, and continue to simmer for 5 more minutes. Turn off the heat and leave covered until ready to serve.

Nutritional yeast (optional)
Green onions, minced (optional)

Sprinkle yeast and green onions over each serving as a garnish.

Per 2 cups: Calories: 267, Protein: 13 gm., Fat: 4 gm., Carbohydrates: 45 gm.

Lentil 'N Barley Soup with Greens

Yield: 10 cups

8 cups water
1 cup lentils
1 cup barley
2 bay leaves

Bring the the water, lentils, barley, and bay leaves to a simmer in a medium soup pot, cover, and cook for 30 minutes. Be sure the heat is low enough that the contents don't boil over.

1 cup chopped green onions
3 cloves garlic, minced
4 packed cups chopped fresh spinach
1 cup chopped asparagus, cut in
    1-inch pieces
½ cup chopped fresh dill
½ tsp salt
¼ cup soy sauce
½ tsp thyme

Add the remaining ingredients to the soup, and cook for 15 more minutes. The lentils should be soft. The barley will still be chewy when you turn off the heat. Cover and let set for several minutes before serving.

Per 2 cups: Calories: 221, Protein: 12 gm., Fat: 0 gm., Carbohydrates: 41 gm.

Seitan Pasta Delight

Yield: 14 cups

This soup is thick like a stew and full of many good flavors. It will remind you of a chicken soup, especially with the chewy seitan nuggets.

1 cup instant gluten flour (vital wheat gluten)
1½ tsp garlic powder
2 tsp dry mustard
1 tsp paprika
¼ tsp black pepper
1 Tbsp soy sauce
1 Tbsp tahini
⅔ cup water

In a small mixing bowl, mix the gluten flour with the garlic powder, dry mustard, paprika, and black pepper. Add the soy sauce, tahini, and ⅔ cup water. Mix with a spoon until a solid mass is formed, then finish mixing with your hands. Roll out into a foot-long log. Cut the log in half lengthwise, then cut each half into thirds lengthwise so you have 6 long, skinny strips. Line them up together and cut cross sections of ¼-inch pieces.

6 cups water

In a large saucepan, simmer the seitan pieces in 6 cups of water for 30 minutes. Stir a few times to keep the nuggets from sticking to each other. They swell during cooking.

1 green pepper, chopped

2 small zucchinis, chopped into ¼-inch rounds

2 cups chopped green onions

2 cups chopped celery (stalks and leaves)

3 cups chopped fresh shiitake mushrooms

3 cups chopped cabbage

1 tsp canola oil

While the seitan is steaming, sauté the green pepper, zucchini, green onions, celery, shiitakes, and cabbage in the oil in a large soup pot for 10 minutes. Stir occasionally to prevent the soup from sticking to the bottom of the pot. After the seitan has finished cooking for 30 minutes, add the entire pot of seitan and the cooking water to the soup pot.

2 cups spiral pasta

4 cups boiling water

Add the pasta and boiling water to the soup pot, and cook for 8-10 minutes.

¾ cup chopped fresh parsley

¼ cup soy sauce

1 Tbsp crushed dried basil

Add the parsley, soy sauce, and basil, and cook for 5-10 more minutes.

½ cup nutritional yeast

Turn off the heat and add the nutritional yeast. Mix well and cover until ready to serve.

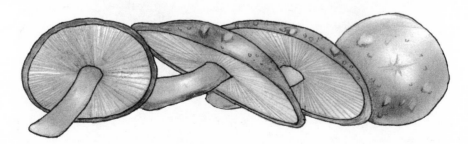

Per 2 cups: Calories: 287, Protein: 28 gm., Fat: 3 gm., Carbohydrates: 38 gm.

Cauliflower Parsley Soup

Yield: 7 cups

The mild, pleasant flavor of this soup makes it perfect for a lunch with sweet muffins.

6 cups water
1 head cauliflower, broken into
**   bite-size pieces (4-5 cups)**

Bring the water and cauliflower to a boil, lower the heat, and simmer for 3 minutes.

1½ cups chopped celery
1 cup chopped scallions
1 cup chopped fresh parsley

Add the celery, scallions, and parsley, and simmer for 5 more minutes.

¼ cup unbleached white flour
¼ cup water
¼ tsp grated nutmeg
½ tsp salt

Make a paste from the flour and water, and add it to the soup. Add the nutmeg and salt, and simmer for 5 minutes. Remove from the heat and cover until ready to serve.

Per 2 cups: Calories: 74, Protein: 3 gm., Fat: 0 gm., Carbohydrates: 15 gm.

Chinese Sour Soup

Yield: 9 cups

You'll enjoy the flavor of ginger and the crunch of the mung beans in this quick soup.

6 cups stock or water
1 lb firm tofu, grated
8 oz fresh mushrooms, chopped
½ tsp salt
3 Tbsp soy sauce

Bring the stock to a boil, and add the tofu, mushrooms, salt, and soy sauce. Simmer for 5 minutes while you prepare the next batch of ingredients.

3 cups mung bean sprouts, rinsed
2 Tbsp shredded gingerroot
3 Tbsp vinegar
¼ tsp black pepper
3 green onions, chopped

Add the bean sprouts, ginger, vinegar, black pepper, and green onions. Cook for 3 minutes from the time the ingredients are added (not from when it reaches a boil).

2 Tbsp cornstarch
¼ cup water

Dissolve the cornstarch in the ¼ cup water, and add it to the soup. Return to a low boil, and cook for 1 minute. Turn off the heat.

1 tsp toasted sesame oil

Add the toasted sesame oil after the heat has been turned off, mix well, and serve.

Per 2 cups: Calories: 144, Protein: 11 gm., Fat: 5 gm., Carbohydrates: 13 gm.

Curried Bok Choy & Snow Pea Soup

Yield: 13 cups

The blend of these spices, especially Indian hing, makes for an enticing soup you'll want to share with friends.

2 tsp cumin
2 tsp coriander
1 tsp turmeric
1 tsp cardamom
2 tsp garam masala (see page 62)
Pinch of cayenne pepper

In a small bowl, mix the spices so they'll be ready to add to the popping seeds.

1 tsp black mustard seeds
1 tsp cumin seeds
⅓ cup minced garlic
Pinch of hing
1 Tbsp canola oil

In the bottom of a large soup pot, heat the seeds, garlic, and hing in the oil, while stirring, until the seeds pop. Add the mixed spices. Lower the heat, stir quickly, and cover the pot so the hot pepper doesn't burn your eyes. Cook for 1 minute or less.

1 cup scallions, chopped
1 head bok choy, chopped (6 cups)
1 eggplant, cubed (4 cups)
1 Tbsp sesame seeds
9 cups hot water
2 cups whole snow peas, washed
½ cup white rice

Add the scallions, bok choy, eggplant, sesame seeds, water, snow peas and rice. Bring to a simmer and cook for 15 minutes.

1 (16-oz) can butter beans, drained
1 tsp salt

Add the beans and salt, return to a simmer, then turn off the heat. Leave covered until ready to serve.

Per 2 cups: Calories: 177, Protein: 7 gm., Fat: 2 gm., Carbohydrates: 30 gm.

East African Peanut Soup

Yield: 8 cups

Make this as spicy as you like, but make it. You will be rewarded with unusual flavors for your efforts.

1 cup raw, unsalted peanuts
½ tsp cardamom seeds
1 tsp black mustard seeds
1 tsp cumin seeds
1 Tbsp sesame seeds
3 Tbsp poppy seeds

Grind the peanuts and seeds in a blender. In a soup pot, stir the blended peanuts and seeds over medium heat until they smell roasted.

1 Tbsp grated gingerroot
1-2 tsp crushed hot pepper flakes
1 tsp salt
4 cups fresh or frozen corn
5 cups water

Add the gingerroot, hot pepper flakes, salt, corn, and water to the soup pot. Bring to a boil, reduce the heat, and simmer for 10 minutes.

½ cup couscous

Add the couscous and continue to simmer for 10 more minutes. Turn off the heat and enjoy. Serve with Dabo Kola (page 117).

Per cup: Calories: 231, Protein: 8 gm., Fat: 10 gm., Carbohydrates: 27 gm.

Green & White Soup

Yield 10 cups

6 cups water
4 cups finely chopped potatoes
4 cups quartered brussels sprouts (1 pound)
1 cup chopped celery (3 stalks)

In a medium soup pot, bring the water to a boil, and add the potatoes, brussels sprouts, and celery. Simmer for 15 minutes.

2 cups green onions, chopped
8 oz water chestnuts, sliced and coarsely chopped
¼ cup grated horseradish
¼ cup soy sauce
½ tsp salt (optional)

Add the green onions, water chestnuts, horseradish, soy sauce, and salt to the soup, and simmer for another 5 minutes. Cover, remove from the heat, and let set a few minutes before serving.

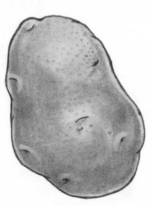

Per 2 cups: Calories: 195, Protein: 4 gm., Fat: 0 gm., Carbohydrates: 43 gm.

Kale Tofu Soup

Yield: 10 cups

1 lb tofu, cubed
2 Tbsp soy sauce
1 large onion, chopped
1 tsp olive oil

In a soup pot, sauté the tofu, soy sauce, and onion in the oil. Cook until browned, stirring frequently to prevent sticking.

8 cups water
4 cups finely chopped kale
2 Tbsp chopped fresh dill, or
**　1 tsp dried**
1 tsp garlic powder

Add the water, kale, dill, and garlic to the soup pot, and boil until the kale is tender, about 10-15 minutes.

2 cups cooked brown rice
¼ cup fresh lemon juice (about
**　2 lemons)**
1 tsp soy sauce

Add the cooked rice, lemon juice, and soy sauce, and bring to a boil. Turn off the heat, cover, and let set for several minutes before serving.

Variation: You may also make this soup with white rice or millet. Add ¾ cup of raw white rice or millet with the kale, and cook for 20 minutes.

Per 2 cups: Calories: 227, Protein: 11 gm., Fat: 6 gm., Carbohydrates: 31 gm.

Lemon Cabbage Soup

Yield: 9 cups

2 Tbsp chopped garlic
1 tsp olive oil

In a soup pot, sauté the garlic in the oil.

5 cups water
3 cups finely chopped potatoes

Add the water and potatoes, and bring to a boil. Cook for 5 minutes.

4 cups finely chopped cabbage
½ pound firm tofu, cut into ¼-inch cubes
1 tsp thyme

Add the cabbage, tofu, and thyme, and return to a boil. Lower the heat and simmer for 5 minutes.

⅔ cup lemon juice
¼ cup liquid aminos or soy sauce

Add the lemon juice and liquid aminos. Simmer a few more minutes, and serve.

Per 2 cups: Calories: 172, Protein: 5 gm., Fat: 2 gm., Carbohydrates: 30 gm.

Roasted Red Pepper Soup

Yield: 14 cups (including dumplings)

Roasting peppers and garlic is easy, and it imparts a unique flavor to this soup. The dumplings are fun to serve; they remind me of matzo balls.

3 red peppers
1 head of garlic

Preheat the oven to 375°F. To roast the peppers and garlic, place them on a cookie sheet, and put them in the oven for 45-60 minutes. (The garlic may take less time to roast than the peppers.) Each garlic clove will become soft and can be squeezed out of its skin after roasting. Turn the peppers several times during the roasting so all sides become charred. Remove the peppers when charred all over, and put into a plastic bag for 10-15 minutes. Remove the outer skins. You can break apart the peppers to remove the seeds, rinsing them under cold water.

1 lb tofu, cut into small cubes
1 medium onion, chopped
8 oz mushrooms, chopped
1 tsp olive oil
1 Tbsp soy sauce

While the peppers and garlic are roasting, sauté the tofu, onion, and mushrooms in the olive oil and soy sauce in a large soup pot. Stir until browned.

10 cups water or stock

Cut the red peppers into bite-sized strips. Add the water or stock and the roasted peppers to the soup pot. Squeeze the garlic into the the soup, and bring to a boil.

2 cups frozen corn
1½ Tbsp dried dill weed
Salt, to taste (optional)

Add the corn, dill weed, and salt to the boiling soup. Lower the heat and simmer for several minutes. Add Sage Dumplings (see recipe below) right before you're ready to serve the soup. If you are not ready to serve the soup yet, turn it off and leave covered until it is time to cook the dumplings.

Per 2 cups with dumplings: Calories: 211, Protein: 9 gm., Fat: 6 gm., Carbohydrates: 31 gm.

Sage Dumplings (12 dumplings):

1 cup unbleached white flour
2 Tbsp barley flour
½ tsp salt
1 tsp baking powder
½ tsp dried sage

Stir the dry ingredients in a small bowl.

1 Tbsp oil
½ cup water

Add the oil and water, and stir well until a sticky batter is formed. Be sure the soup stock is at a low boil, and drop the batter quickly, by tablespoonfuls, into the soup. Cover the soup while the dumplings simmer for 1½ minutes. Remove the lid and turn the dumplings over with a slotted spoon. Return the lid to the pot. Cook another 1½ minutes, then remove the soup from the heat. Serve several dumplings in each bowl with lots of the colorful vegetables and tofu to surround them.

Per dumpling: Calories: 48, Protein: 1 gm., Fat: 1 gm., Carbohydrates: 8 gm.

Shiitake Soybean Soup

Yield: 14 cups

2 cups chopped green onions
4 cups chopped fresh shiitake mushrooms
2 tsp canola oil

In a large soup pot, sauté the green onions and shiitakes in the canola oil until they are soft and a thick, saucy stock has developed.

7 cups water
4 cups chopped kale, collards, Swiss chard, or spinach

Add the water and greens, and bring to a boil. Lower the heat and simmer for 10 minutes.

3 cups cooked soybeans
3 cups cooked rice
2 tsp garam masala*
1 Tbsp Jamaican curry**
⅓ cup soy sauce

Add the soybeans, rice, spices, and soy sauce. Return to an active simmer, and cook for 5 minutes. Remove from the heat.

1 tsp toasted sesame oil

Add the sesame oil, mix well, and cover until ready to serve.

*Garam masala is a sweet spice mix. It can be purchased already mixed or you can make your own by using equal amounts of cinnamon, cloves, and cardamom.

**Jamaican curry is a mix of turmeric, fenugreek, coriander, cumin, anise, star anise, pepper, pimento, cloves, and garlic.

Per cup: Calories: 331, Protein: 17 gm., Fat: 9 gm., Carbohydrates: 45 gm.

Muffins

Muffins are wonderful, instant accompaniments to soup with enough variations to keep you as the cook, as well as your eaters, from getting bored with the "same ole thing." Here's a few tips for making successful muffins with the least amount of effort.

• Mix muffin batter well but don't overbeat.

• Mix your wet ingredients together, then sift or add your dry ingredients, and mix until all the liquid is absorbed by the flours. Add additional fruit, nuts, or chopped vegetables last.

• Lightly oil your muffin tins, especially the bottoms. The sides hardly need any.

• After baking your muffins, put the tins out on a cake rack to cool. Don't try to remove hot muffins from the tins. Let them cool for 5-10 minutes, THEN slide a table knife around the sides, and pry them out. When they are almost cooled down, they pop right out.

• If you're making several batches of muffins at the same time, you don't have to wash your tins between each batch. A few hardened muffin crumbs left on the muffin tin won't effect your next muffins. They will still come loose with gentle prying.

• Baking time will vary depending on the type and size of muffins. I usually rotate my pans 180° after 10 minutes to assure even baking. Test to see if the muffins are done by inserting a toothpick in the middle of a muffin. If the toothpick comes out clean, the muffins are done.

Sweet Muffins

Almond Meal-Buckwheat Muffins

Yield: 12 muffins

Full of nuts and dried fruit, these muffins are a good compliment to Easy Cream of Broccoli Soup (page 45).

Preheat the oven to 350°F.

¾ cup dried fruit (dates, apricots, figs) chopped
1 cup soy yogurt
½ cup almonds, blended into a coarse meal (some chunks are ok)
½ cup sorghum molasses
1 tsp vanilla

Mix together the soy yogurt, dried fruit, almonds, molasses, and vanilla.

Dry Ingredients:
1½ cups unbleached white flour
1 cup buckwheat flour
1 tsp baking powder
1 tsp baking soda
½ tsp salt

Sift the dry ingredients into the nut/fruit mixture. Mix well and spoon into lightly oiled muffin tins until they are ⅔ full. Bake for 15-18 minutes.

Test to see if the muffins are done by inserting a toothpick in the middle of a muffin. If the toothpick comes out clean, the muffins are done.

Per muffin: Calories: 185, Protein: 4 gm., Fat: 3 gm., Carbohydrates: 33 gm.

Amaranth-Lemon-Apple Muffins

Yield: 12 muffins

These are chewy muffins with a distinct flavor.

Preheat the oven to 350°F.

1 apple, grated
½ cup raisins
½ cup brown sugar
½ cup fresh lemon juice
3 Tbsp canola oil

In a medium mixing bowl, stir the apple, raisins, sugar, lemon juice, and oil until thoroughly combined.

Dry Ingredients:
1¾ cups unbleached wheat flour
½ cup amaranth flour
1 tsp baking powder
1 tsp baking soda
½ tsp salt
¼ tsp ground cloves

Sift the dry ingredients into the liquid ingredients, and stir everything together until all the dry ingredients are absorbed. Spoon into lightly oiled muffin tins, and bake for 18 minutes.

Test to see if the muffins are done by inserting a toothpick in the middle of a muffin. If the toothpick comes out clean, the muffins are done.

Per muffin: Calories: 156, Protein: 3 gm., Fat: 3 gm., Carbohydrates: 28 gm.

Applesauce Raisin Muffins

Yield: 12 muffins

Preheat the oven to 350°F.

Liquid Ingredients:
1 cup applesauce
½ cup orange juice
2 Tbsp oil
2 Tbsp liquid sweetener
1 Tbsp brown sugar

Mix the liquid ingredients in a mixing bowl.

Dry Ingredients:
2 cups flour
1½ tsp baking soda
½ tsp cinnamon
¼ tsp salt

Sift the dry ingredients into the liquid ingredients. Stir well but don't overbeat.

½ cup raisins

Add the raisins and mix them in just before spooning the muffins into lightly oiled muffin tins. Bake for 18-20 minutes.

Test to see if the muffins are done by inserting a toothpick in the middle of a muffin. If the toothpick comes out clean, the muffins are done.

Per muffin: Calories: 114, Protein: 2 gm., Fat: 2 gm., Carbohydrates: 20 gm.

Banana Muffins

Yield: 12 muffins

These are large muffins—just the recipe for those ripe bananas!

Preheat the oven to 350°F.

In a mixing bowl, combine the liquid ingredients and mix well.

Liquid Ingredients:
1¼ cups mashed, ripe bananas
  (3 bananas)
½ cup liquid sweetener
2-4 Tbsp canola oil
2 Tbsp orange juice
1 Tbsp blackstrap molasses
1 Tbsp brown sugar (optional)

Dry Ingredients:
2½ cups unbleached white flour
1 tsp baking powder
½ tsp baking soda
½ tsp salt

Sift the dry ingredients into the liquid ingredients, and mix thoroughly.

½ cup raisins

Add the raisins and stir just enough to evenly distribute them. Fill lightly oiled muffin tins, and bake for 18 minutes.

Test to see if the muffins are done by inserting a toothpick in the middle of a muffin. If the toothpick comes out clean, the muffins are done.

Per muffin: Calories: 201, Protein: 3 gm., Fat: 3 gm., Carbohydrates: 39 gm.

Cake Muffins

Yield: 10 plain muffins (12 fruit and nut muffins)

I have Jenna to thank for sharing this recipe with us. These muffins melt in your mouth. There are many variations you can play with depending on your mood.

Preheat the oven to 350°F.

Dry Ingredients:
1½ **cups flour**
1 **tsp baking soda**
½ **tsp baking powder**
¼ **tsp salt**

Mix the dry ingredients in a medium mixing bowl.

Liquid Ingredients:
¾ **cup water**
½ **cup liquid sweetener**
3 **Tbsp canola oil**
1 **tsp vanilla**

Add the liquid ingredients to the dry ingredients, and mix thoroughly. If you are going to add fruit, nuts, or herbs for any of the variations listed below, do it now. Pour the batter into lightly oiled muffin tins, and bake for 15-20 minutes.

Per muffin: Calories: 148, Protein: 2 gm., Fat: 3 gm., Carbohydrates: 26 gm.

Variations:
½ **cup dried fruit**
½ **cup nuts or seeds**
½ **cup corn and onions**
1 **Tbsp poppy or sesame seeds**
1 **Tbsp herbs, fresh or dried**
1 **Tbsp grated fresh ginger, or** ½ **tsp powdered**
1 **tsp lemon or orange zest**

Add 1 or 2 of these (You may want to omit the vanilla.)

Test to see if the muffins are done by inserting a toothpick in the middle of a muffin. If the toothpick comes out clean, the muffins are done.

Carrot-Barley Flour Muffins

Yield: 12 muffins

Preheat the oven to 350°F.

Mix together the liquid ingredients.

Liquid Ingredients:
1 cup grated carrot
¾ cup pineapple juice
¼ cup liquid sweetener
2 Tbsp oil
1 tsp vanilla

Dry Ingredients:
1½ cups unbleached white flour
1 cup barley flour
½ cup chopped pecans (optional)
1 tsp baking powder
1 tsp baking soda
¼ tsp salt

Sift the dry ingredients into the liquid ingredients, and stir well. Spoon into lightly oiled muffin tins, and bake for 18 minutes.

Test to see if the muffins are done by inserting a toothpick in the middle of a muffin. If the toothpick comes out clean, the muffins are done.

Per muffin: Calories: 137, Protein: 3 gm., Fat: 2 gm., Carbohydrates: 26 gm.

Datey Flax Seed Muffins

Yield: 12 muffins

Preheat the oven to 350°F.

3 Tbsp flax seeds
1¼ cups orange juice

In a blender, whip up the flax seeds and orange juice, then pour into a mixing bowl.

2 Tbsp canola oil
3 Tbsp liquid sweetener
1½ cups chopped dates

Add the oil, liquid sweetener, and dates to the bowl with the flax seed/orange juice mix. Mix all the ingredients together.

1 cup unbleached white flour
1 cup whole wheat flour
½ cup barley flour
2 tsp baking power
1 tsp baking soda
½ tsp salt

Sift the white flour, whole wheat flour, barley flour, baking powder, and baking soda, and salt into the liquid ingredients, and mix well. Pour into lightly oiled muffin tins, and bake for 15 minutes.

Test to see if the muffins are done by inserting a toothpick in the middle of a muffin. If the toothpick comes out clean, the muffins are done.

Per muffin: Calories: 204, Protein: 4 gm., Fat: 3 gm., Carbohydrates: 40 gm.

Granola Muffins

Yield: 12 muffins

These muffins use the oil from the granola, so no oil is added to the batter. These are good with a fruit preserve.

Preheat the oven to 350°F.

1 overripe banana, mashed (⅓ cup)
1 cup granola
1 cup soy yogurt
⅓ cup orange juice
2 Tbsp liquid sweetener

Mash the banana in a mixing bowl, and then add the granola, soy yogurt, orange juice, and liquid sweetener.

Dry Ingredients:
1¼ cups unbleached white flour
¾ cup brown rice flour
2 tsp baking powder
¼ tsp salt

Sift the dry ingredients into the liquid ingredients, and mix well. Spoon into lightly oiled muffin tins, and bake for 15 minutes. Don't overbake.

Test to see if the muffins are done by inserting a toothpick in the middle of a muffin. If the toothpick comes out clean, the muffins are done.

Per muffin: Calories: 155, Protein: 4 gm., Fat: 4 gm., Carbohydrates: 28 gm.

Kiwi Ginger Muffins

Yield: 12 muffins

These large, puffy muffins are full of fruity, ginger-flavored goodness.

Preheat the oven to 350°F.

8 kiwi, mashed (1½ cups)
½ cup cooked oatmeal

Mash the kiwi and oatmeal into a smooth paste.

3 Tbsp oil
½ cup sorghum molasses
1-1½ Tbsp grated gingerroot

Add the oil, molasses, and ginger-root to the kiwi, and stir well.

Dry Ingredients:
3 cups unbleached white flour (or
 substitute some whole wheat)
2 tsp baking power
1 tsp baking soda
½ tsp salt

Add the dry ingredients to the kiwi mixture, and mix well. Spoon into lightly oiled muffin tins, filling each until nearly full. Bake for 20 minutes.

Test to see if the muffins are done by inserting a toothpick in the middle of a muffin. If the toothpick comes out clean, the muffins are done.

Per muffin: Calories: 215, Protein: 4 gm., Fat: 3 gm., Carbohydrates: 41 gm.

Lemon Blueberry Muffins

Yield: 12 muffins

These sweet, tangy muffins will please your taste buds.

Preheat the oven to 350°F.

Liquid Ingredients:
⅔ **cup lemon juice**
1 ripe banana, mashed
¼ **cup soy yogurt**
3 Tbsp oil

Mix the liquid ingredients in a medium mixing bowl.

Dry Ingredients:
2 cups unbleached white flour
¾ **cup oat bran**
⅔ **cup granulated sweetener**
1½ tsp baking soda
½ **tsp salt**

Sift the dry ingredients into the liquid ingredients. Stir well until all the dry ingredients are absorbed.

1 cup fresh blueberries or frozen blueberries, thawed

Add the blueberries and mix gently so as to not crush the berries. Fill lightly oiled muffin tins full, and bake for 18 minutes.

Test to see if the muffins are done by inserting a toothpick in the middle of a muffin. If the toothpick comes out clean, the muffins are done.

Per muffin: Calories: 158, Protein: 2 gm., Fat: 3 gm., Carbohydrates: 29 gm.

Lime Muffins

Yield: 12 muffins

These muffins are pungent with lime flavor. Use fresh lime juice for best results.

Preheat the oven to 350°F.

¾ cup roasted sunflower seeds

In a dry skillet, roast the sunflower seeds while stirring to prevent the seeds from burning. Set aside to add to the batter later.

Liquid Ingredients:
1 cup lime juice
½ cup liquid sweetener
½ cup granulated sweetener
¼ cup orange juice
2 Tbsp canola oil
1 tsp vanilla

Mix together the liquid ingredients.

Dry Ingredients:
2 cups unbleached white flour
1 cup barley flour
1 tsp baking powder
1 tsp baking soda
½ tsp salt

Sift the dry ingredients into the liquid ingredients. Stir gently and add the roasted sunflower seeds to the batter. Spoon immediately into lightly oiled muffin tins, filling the cups nearly full. Bake for 18-20 minutes.

Test to see if the muffins are done by inserting a toothpick in the middle of a muffin. If the toothpick comes out clean, the muffins are done.

Per muffin: Calories: 234, Protein: 5 gm., Fat: 7 gm., Carbohydrates: 37 gm.

Mango Muffins

Yield: 12 muffins

Working with mangoes can be messy, but good things don't always come easily. These orange muffins are ones you'll be proud to serve.

Preheat the oven to 350°F.

Pulp of 2 ripe mangoes (1⅓ cups)

To get the pulp off the mango, slit it in half the long way. Twist it open and scrape the pulp off the seed and away from the skin with a spoon.

2 Tbsp cooked oatmeal
½ cup orange juice

In a food processor, blend the mango pulp, oatmeal, and orange juice. Transfer the mixture to a mixing bowl.

½ cup sorghum molasses or liquid sweetener
3 Tbsp canola oil
½ tsp vanilla

Add the molasses, oil, and vanilla to the bowl, and mix well.

Dry Ingredients:
2 cups unbleached white flour
½ cup barley flour
¾ cup raisins (optional)
1 tsp baking powder
1 tsp baking soda
½ tsp salt

Sift the dry ingredients into the liquid ingredients, and blend well. Add the raisins and fold in. Fill lightly oiled muffin tins full to use all the batter. Bake for 20 minutes.

Test to see if the muffins are done by inserting a toothpick in the middle of a muffin. If the toothpick comes out clean, the muffins are done.

Per muffin: Calories: 188, Protein: 3 gm., Fat: 3 gm., Carbohydrates: 36 gm.

Oatmeal Muffins

Yield: 12 muffins

Preheat the oven to 350°F.

Liquid Ingredients:
1 cup nondairy milk
½ cup soy yogurt
⅓ cup liquid sweetener
3 Tbsp canola oil
1 Tbsp blackstrap molasses
1 tsp vanilla

In a mixing bowl, combine the liquid ingredients.

1 cup unbleached white flour
1 cup whole wheat flour
1 tsp baking powder
½ tsp baking soda
½ tsp salt
1 cup quick or regular rolled oats

Sift the white flour, wheat flour, baking powder, baking soda, and salt into the liquid ingredients, add the oatmeal, and stir well.

1 cup raisins

Add the raisins and gently mix. Spoon the batter into lightly oiled muffin tins, and bake for 15 minutes.

Test to see if the muffins are done by inserting a toothpick in the middle of a muffin. If the toothpick comes out clean, the muffins are done.

Per muffin: Calories: 203, Protein: 4 gm., Fat: 5 gm., Carbohydrates: 35 gm.

Orange Sweet Potato Muffins

Yield: 12 muffins

These orange muffins are colorful, tasty, and good with Rutabaga & Mushroom Soup (page 33).

Preheat the oven to 350°F.

¾ cup cooked, mashed sweet potatoes (baked or boiled)
2 Tbsp canola oil
2 Tbsp liquid sweetener
1 cup orange juice (freshly squeezed is best)

Combine the mashed sweet potatoes, oil, liquid sweetener, and juice in a mixing bowl, and mix well.

Dry Ingredients:
1¾ cups unbleached flour
1½ tsp baking powder
½ tsp baking soda
¼ tsp salt

Sift the dry ingredients into the liquid ingredients, and stir until well blended. Spoon into lightly oiled muffin tins, and bake for 15 minutes.

Test to see if the muffins are done by inserting a toothpick in the middle of a muffin. If the toothpick comes out clean, the muffins are done.

Per muffin: Calories: 108, Protein: 2 gm., Fat: 2 gm., Carbohydrates: 20 gm.

Pineapple-Date-Nut Muffins

Yield: 12 muffins

Chock full of fruit, try these with Easy Cream of Broccoli Soup (page 45).

Preheat the oven to 350°F.

1 banana, mashed
½ cup crushed pineapple
½ cup chopped dates
½ cup chopped walnuts
½ cup orange juice
2 Tbsp canola oil
2 Tbsp liquid sweetener

Mix the banana, pineapple, dates, walnuts, juice, oil, and liquid sweetener in a mixing bowl.

Dry Ingredients:
2 cups unbleached white flour
1 tsp baking powder
1 tsp baking soda
½ tsp salt

Sift the dry ingredients into the liquid ingredients, and mix until all the liquid has been absorbed. Spoon into lightly oiled muffin tins, and bake for 20 minutes.

Test to see if the muffins are done by inserting a toothpick in the middle of a muffin. If the toothpick comes out clean, the muffins are done.

Per muffin: Calories: 161, Protein: 3 gm., Fat: 5 gm., Carbohydrates: 25 gm.

Rhubarb Raspberry-Filled Muffins

Yield: 12 muffins

The fruit filling creates a marbled effect in these muffins.

Preheat the oven to 350°F.

Rhubarb Raspberry Filling:
1½ cups chopped rhubarb
1 heaping cup fresh or frozen
   raspberries
½ cup sugar

In a medium saucepan, combine the rhubarb, raspberries, and sugar. Cover and cook for 5 minutes. Remove the lid and cook until a thick jam is formed, about 5 more minutes.

Liquid Ingredients:
¾ cup orange juice
½ cup flax seed mixture (page 123)
½ cup nondairy yogurt
¼ cup liquid sweetener
3 Tbsp canola oil

In a blender, whip the liquid ingredients. Pour this creamy liquid into a medium mixing bowl.

Dry Ingredients:
1 cup unbleached white flour
1 cup whole wheat flour
1½ tsp baking powder
1 tsp baking soda
¼ tsp salt

Sift the dry ingredients into the liquid ingredients, and mix well. Spoon 2-3 Tbsp of batter into each lightly oiled muffin tin. They should be only ⅓ full. Spoon 3 Tbsp of the rhubarb/raspberry filling into each partially filled muffin tin. Divide the rest of the batter by spooning it into the muffin tins to cover the berry filling. Fill the muffin tins to the top. Bake for 18-20 minutes.

Test to see if the muffins are done by inserting a toothpick in the middle of a muffin. If the toothpick comes out clean, the muffins are done.

Per muffin: Calories: 173, Protein: 3 gm., Fat: 4 gm., Carbohydrates: 31 gm.

Spicy Zucchini Muffins

Yield: 12 muffins

These muffins are rich, like little cakes. This is a good way to use surplus zucchini when the garden is pumping them out.

Preheat the oven to 350°F.

¼ **cup canola oil**
¾ **cup liquid sweetener**
1 **Tbsp blackstrap molasses**
2 **cups grated zucchini**

In a mixing bowl, stir together the oil, liquid sweetener, molasses, and zucchini.

Dry Ingredients:
2 **cups white flour**
1 **cup whole wheat flour**
1 **tsp powdered ginger**
1 **tsp cinnamon**
1 **tsp baking soda**
1 **tsp baking powder**
½ **tsp salt**

Sift the dry ingredients into the liquid ingredients, and stir until blended.

½ **cup raisins**

Mix in the raisins and spoon into lightly oiled muffin tins until they are full. Bake for 20 minutes.

Test to see if the muffins are done by inserting a toothpick in the middle of a muffin. If the toothpick comes out clean, the muffins are done.

Per muffin: Calories: 212, Protein: 3 gm., Fat: 5 gm., Carbohydrates: 39 gm.

Strawberry Almond Muffins

Yield: 12 muffins

Preheat the oven to 350°F.

Liquid Ingredients:
1 cup nondairy milk
½ cup granulated sweetener
2 Tbsp oil
2 Tbsp sorghum molasses
2 Tbsp orange juice
½ tsp vanilla

In a medium mixing bowl, combine the liquid ingredients, and stir until everything is well blended.

Dry Ingredients:
2 cups unbleached white flour
½ cup barley flour
¼ cup wheat germ
1 tsp baking soda
1 tsp baking powder
¼ tsp salt

Sift the dry ingredients into the liquid ingredients, and stir until the dry ingredients are well blended.

1 cup fresh strawberries, chopped into chunks (frozen and thawed will work too)
½ cup roasted almonds, chopped

Add the strawberries and almonds to the batter, and mix well. Fill lightly oiled muffin tins, and bake for 15 minutes.

Test to see if the muffins are done by inserting a toothpick in the middle of a muffin. If the toothpick comes out clean, the muffins are done.

Per muffin: Calories: 203, Protein: 5 gm., Fat: 7 gm., Carbohydrates: 32 gm.

Sunflower Seed-Orange Muffins

Yield: 12 muffins

Preheat the oven to 350°F.

¾ cup roasted sunflower seeds

Blend the roasted sunflower seeds into a coarse meal. Set aside to add with the dry ingredients.

Liquid Ingredients:
1¼ cups freshly squeezed orange juice
¼ cup liquid sweetener
2 Tbsp oil

In a medium mixing bowl, combine the liquid ingredients.

Dry Ingredients:
1 cup unbleached white flour
¾ cup rice flour
1 tsp baking powder
1 tsp baking soda
½ tsp salt

Sift the dry ingredients into the liquid ingredients, and add the sunflower seed meal. Mix well and spoon into lightly oiled muffin tins. Bake for 15 minutes.

Test to see if the muffins are done by inserting a toothpick in the middle of a muffin. If the toothpick comes out clean, the muffins are done.

Per muffin: Calories: 169, Protein: 4 gm., Fat: 7 gm., Carbohydrates: 23 gm.

Sweet Potato-Pineapple Muffins

Yield: 12 muffins

Preheat the oven to 350°F.

Liquid Ingredients:
¾ **cup mashed sweet potatoes**
¾ **cup pineapple juice**
½ **cup crushed pineapple, drained**
   (save the juice)
2 **Tbsp canola oil**
2 **Tbsp maple syrup**

Combine the liquid ingredients in a mixing bowl, and mix well.

Dry Ingredients:
2 **cups unbleached white flour**
1½ **tsp ground ginger**
1 **tsp baking powder**
1 **tsp baking soda**
¼ **tsp salt**

Sift the dry ingredients into the liquid ingredients, and stir well. Spoon into lightly oiled muffin tins, and bake for 20 minutes.

Test to see if the muffins are done by inserting a toothpick in the middle of a muffin. If the toothpick comes out clean, the muffins are done.

Per muffin: Calories: 116, Protein: 2 gm., Fat: 2 gm., Carbohydrates: 21 gm.

Tropical Muffins

Yield: 12 muffins

Preheat the oven to 350°F.

Liquid Ingredients:
1 banana, mashed
¾ cup coconut milk
½ cup lime juice

Mix the liquid ingredients in a medium mixing bowl.

Dry Ingredients:
1 cup unbleached white flour
¾ cup whole wheat flour
¾ cup wheat germ
¾ cup granulated sweetener
1 tsp baking powder
1 tsp baking soda
¼ tsp salt

Mix the dry ingredients to the liquid ingredients, and stir well. Spoon into lightly oiled muffin tins, fill ⅔ full, and bake for 18 minutes.

Test to see if the muffins are done by inserting a toothpick in the middle of a muffin. If the toothpick comes out clean, the muffins are done.

Per muffin: Calories: 141, Protein: 4 gm., Fat: 4 gm., Carbohydrates: 19 gm.

Very Berry Muffins

Yield: 12 muffins

These muffins are light and full of berries.

Preheat the oven to 350°F.

Liquid Ingredients:
1 cup nondairy milk
½ cup flax seed mixture (page 123)
½ cup liquid sweetener
3 Tbsp canola oil
1 tsp vanilla

In a blender, combine the liquid ingredients. Blend until smooth and creamy, and pour into a mixing bowl.

Dry Ingredients:
1½ cups unbleached white flour
½ cup barley flour
½ cup whole wheat flour
1½ tsp baking powder
1 tsp baking soda
¼ tsp salt

Sift the dry ingredients into the liquid ingredients, and stir until all the dry ingredients are absorbed.

2 cups berries: raspberries,
blackberries, strawberries, etc.
(fresh or frozen and thawed)

Gently stir the berries into the muffin batter. Spoon into lightly oiled muffin tins, and bake for 20 minutes.

Test to see if the muffins are done by inserting a toothpick in the middle of a muffin. If the toothpick comes out clean, the muffins are done.

Per muffin: Calories: 179, Protein: 3 gm., Fat: 4 gm., Carbohydrates: 31 gm.

Wheatless Muffins

Yield: 12 muffins

You won't miss the wheat in these tasty muffins.

Preheat the oven to 375°F.

Dry Ingredients:
1½ cups barley flour
1 cup oat flour
1 cup cornmeal
3 tsp baking powder
½ tsp baking soda
½ tsp salt
¼ tsp cinnamon

Mix the dry ingredients in a medium mixing bowl.

½ cup flax seed mixture (page 123)

1⅓ cups nondairy milk
½ cup liquid sweetener
2 Tbsp canola oil

Add the flax seed mixture, liquid sweetener, oil, and nondairy milk, to the dry ingredients. Stir well enough to dissolve all the dry ingredients.

½ cup raisins
½ cup sunflower seeds

Mix in the raisins and sunflower seeds. Spoon into lightly oiled muffin tins, and bake for 18 minutes.

Test to see if the muffins are done by inserting a toothpick in the middle of a muffin. If the toothpick comes out clean, the muffins are done.

Per muffin: Calories: 126, Protein: 6 gm., Fat: 7 gm., Carbohydrates: 42 gm.

Savory Muffins
Corny Olive Muffins

Yield: 12 muffins

Preheat the oven to 350°F.

1 cup nondairy milk
2 Tbsp oil
2 Tbsp liquid sweetener
1 cup corn (canned, drained, or
  frozen, briefly cooked)
36 chopped stuffed green olives,
  (½ cup)

In a medium mixing bowl, stir together the nondairy milk, oil, liquid sweetener, corn, and olives.

Dry Ingredients:
1 cup white flour
1 cup cornmeal
2 tsp baking powder
1 tsp cumin

Sift the dry ingredients into the liquid ingredients. Stir until blended and spoon into muffin tins. Bake for 18 minutes.

Test to see if the muffins are done by inserting a toothpick in the middle of a muffin. If the toothpick comes out clean, the muffins are done.

Per muffin: Calories: 135, Protein: 3 gm., Fat: 3 gm., Carbohydrates: 22 gm.

Couscous Herb Muffins

Yield: 12 muffins

These muffins taste like Thanksgiving stuffing.

Preheat the oven to 375°F.

1 medium onion, chopped
1 tsp canola oil
1 Tbsp soy sauce

Sauté the onion in the oil and soy sauce until soft.

2 Tbsp canola oil
1 Tbsp liquid sweetener
¾ cup cooked couscous
1 cup nondairy milk

In a mixing bowl, mix together the oil, liquid sweetener, couscous, and nondairy milk. Add the sautéed onion.

1 cup unbleached white flour
1 cup whole wheat flour
1½ tsp baking powder
½ tsp baking soda
½ tsp salt
1 tsp crushed rosemary
½ tsp thyme
1 tsp crushed sage

Sift the white flour, wheat flour, baking powder, baking soda, and salt into the bowl of mixed ingredients. Add the rosemary, thyme, and sage, and stir well. Spoon into lightly oiled muffin tins, and bake for 15 minutes.

Test to see if the muffins are done by inserting a toothpick in the middle of a muffin. If the toothpick comes out clean, the muffins are done.

Per muffin: Calories: 36, Protein: 2 gm., Fat: 1 gm., Carbohydrates: 5 gm.

Cranberry Corn Muffins

Yield: 12 muffins

Preheat the oven to 350°F.

Liquid Ingredients:
½ **cup nondairy milk**
½ **cup water**
¼ **cup liquid sweetener**
3 **Tbsp oil**

In a mixing bowl, combine the liquid ingredients, and mix well.

Dry Ingredients:
1 **cup unbleached white flour**
1 **cup cornmeal**
¼ **cup whole wheat flour**
¼ **cup wheat germ**
1 **tsp baking power**
½ **tsp baking soda**
¼ **tsp salt**

Sift the dry ingredients into the liquid ingredients. Stir gently until all the liquid is absorbed.

1¼ **cups washed cranberries**

Mix the cranberries into the muffin batter. Fill lightly oiled muffin tins about ⅔ full, and bake for 15-18 minutes.

Test to see if the muffins are done by inserting a toothpick in the middle of a muffin. If the toothpick comes out clean, the muffins are done.

Per muffin: Calories: 152, Protein: 3 gm., Fat: 3 gm., Carbohydrates: 25 gm.

Kasha Muffins

Yield: 12 muffins

1 cup cooked buckwheat groats (kasha)
½ cup orange-pineapple juice concentrate, thawed
¼ cup liquid sweetener
3 Tbsp canola oil

Dry Ingredients:
2 cups unbleached white flour
1 tsp baking powder
1 tsp baking soda
½ tsp salt

Preheat the oven to 350°F.

Mix the kasha, juice concentrate, sweetener and oil until well blended.

Sift the dry ingredients into the liquid ingredients. Stir until all the liquid has been absorbed. Don't overbeat. Place in lightly oiled muffin tins, and bake for 16-20 minutes. Test to see if the muffins are done by inserting a toothpick in the middle of a muffin. If the toothpick comes out clean, the muffins are done.

Test to see if the muffins are done by inserting a toothpick in the middle of a muffin. If the toothpick comes out clean, the muffins are done.

Per muffin: Calories: 153, Protein: 3 gm., Fat: 3 gm., Carbohydrates: 27 gm.

Mashed Potato and Gravy Muffins

Yield: 12 muffins

Mashed potatoes and gravy is one of my kids' favorite dishes. Now you can make muffins which are moist and chewy with the same ingredients and good flavor.

Preheat the oven to 350°F.

1 cup unbleached white flour
½ cup nutritional yeast

In a dry skillet, toast the flour and nutritional yeast, while stirring, until they are lightly browned and have a roasted aroma.

½ cup mashed potatoes
3 Tbsp canola oil
¼ cup soy sauce
½ cup potato water

¾ cup nondairy milk

In a mixing bowl, mash together with a fork the mashed potatoes, oil, soy sauce, potato water, and nondairy milk. Add the toasted yeast and flour.

1 cup unbleached white flour
2 tsp baking powder
¼ tsp garlic powder
⅛ tsp black pepper

Sift the flour, baking powder, garlic, and black pepper into the other ingredients. Mix well and spoon the batter into lightly oiled muffin tins. Bake for 18 minutes. Test to see if the muffins are done by inserting a toothpick in the middle of a muffin. If the toothpick comes out clean, the muffins are done.

Test to see if the muffins are done by inserting a toothpick in the middle of a muffin. If the toothpick comes out clean, the muffins are done.

Per muffin: Calories: 118, Protein: 3 gm., Fat: 3 gm., Carbohydrates: 19 gm.

Onion-Pepper-Rice Muffins

Yield: 12 muffins

These muffins are moist and tasty.

Preheat the oven to 375°F.

1 onion, finely chopped
1 green pepper, finely chopped
1 tsp olive oil

In a medium skillet, sauté the onion and green pepper in the oil. Stir them until they are browned and soft.

1 cup nondairy milk
1 cup cooked rice
3 Tbsp cooked oatmeal
2 Tbsp canola oil
1 Tbsp liquid sweetener

In a mixing bowl, combine the nondairy milk, rice, oatmeal, oil, and sweetener. Stir well and add the sautéed vegetables.

1 cup unbleached white flour
1 cup whole wheat flour
2 tsp baking powder
½ tsp salt

Sift the white flour, wheat flour, baking powder, and salt into the other ingredients, and stir well. Fill lightly oiled muffin tins to the top. Bake for 18 minutes.

Test to see if the muffins are done by inserting a toothpick in the middle of a muffin. If the toothpick comes out clean, the muffins are done.

Per muffin: Calories: 128, Protein: 3 gm., Fat: 3 gm., Carbohydrates: 21 gm.

Parsnip Lemon Muffins

Yield: 12 muffins

These muffins are moist and chewy. If you aren't familiar with parsnips, you're in for a treat here.

Preheat the oven to 350°F.

⅔ **cup peeled, grated parsnips**
1 **cup hot water**
2 **Tbsp oil**
3 **Tbsp liquid sweetener**
2 **Tbsp lemon juice**

Combine the parsnips, water, oil, liquid sweetener, lemon juice, and in a mixing bowl, and let set for 10 minutes.

Dry Ingredients:
1 **cup unbleached white flour**
½ **cup whole wheat flour**
½ **cup amaranth flour**
1 **tsp baking powder**
1 **tsp baking soda**
¼ **tsp salt**

Sift the dry ingredients into the liquid ingredients. Immediately spoon this batter into lightly oiled muffin tins because the addition of the dry ingredients causes the batter to fluff up. Bake for 20 minutes.

Test to see if the muffins are done by inserting a toothpick in the middle of a muffin. If the toothpick comes out clean, the muffins are done.

Per muffin: Calories: 112, Protein: 2 gm., Fat: 2 gm., Carbohydrates: 19 gm.

Peanut Butter-Oatmeal Muffins

Yield: 12 muffins

These large, chewy muffins are a wholesome snack or accompaniment to soup.

Preheat the oven to 350°F.

1 cup cooked oatmeal
¾ cup peanut butter
1 tsp vanilla
⅔ cup liquid sweetener
1 cup nondairy milk

In a medium mixing bowl, mix the cooked oatmeal with the peanut butter, vanilla, liquid sweetener, and nondairy milk. Stir until all the lumps are gone.

Dry Ingredients:
1 cup whole wheat flour
1 cup unbleached white flour
½ cup barley flour
1 tsp baking soda
1 tsp baking powder
½ tsp salt

Add the dry ingredients to the liquid ingredients, and stir well. Fill lightly oiled muffin tins evenly with batter, and bake for 20 minutes.

Test to see if the muffins are done by inserting a toothpick in the middle of a muffin. If the toothpick comes out clean, the muffins are done.

Per muffin: Calories: 256, Protein: 8 gm., Fat: 8 gm., Carbohydrates: 37 gm.

Rye Muffins with Capers

Yield: 12 muffins

If you like the spicy, salty taste of capers, try this unusual muffin. They are good with a vegetarian cheese-flavored herb spread.

Preheat the oven to 350°F.

Liquid Ingredients:
1 cup nondairy yogurt
⅔ cup water
½ cup unsulphured molasses
3 Tbsp oil

Mix the liquid ingredients in a mixing bowl.

Dry Ingredients:
1½ cups unbleached white flour
1 cup rye flour
½ cup cornmeal
1 tsp baking powder
1 tsp baking soda

Add the dry ingredients to the liquid ingredients, and stir until all the dry ingredients are absorbed.

½ cup drained capers

Add the capers and gently stir into the batter. Fill lightly oiled muffin tins, and bake for 16-18 minutes.

Test to see if the muffins are done by inserting a toothpick in the middle of a muffin. If the toothpick comes out clean, the muffins are done.

Per muffin: Calories: 190, Protein: 3 gm., Fat: 3 gm., Carbohydrates: 35 gm.

Salsa Corn Muffins

Yield: 12 muffins

Preheat the oven to 350°F.

2 cups fresh or canned corn
1 cup hot salsa
1 cup potato water or water
3 Tbsp oil
2 Tbsp liquid sweetener

In a mixing bowl, stir together the corn, salsa, potato water, oil, and liquid sweetener.

Dry Ingredients:
2 cups unbleached white flour
½ cup whole wheat flour
½ cup cornmeal
1 tsp cumin
1 tsp baking powder
1 tsp baking soda
½ tsp garlic powder
½ tsp salt

Sift the dry ingrdients into the bowl of liquid ingredients. Stir well and fill lightly oiled muffin tins full. Bake for 18-20 minutes.

Test to see if the muffins are done by inserting a toothpick in the middle of a muffin. If the toothpick comes out clean, the muffins are done.

Per muffin: Calories: 174, Protein: 4 gm., Fat: 3 gm., Carbohydrates: 31 gm.

Spiced Buckwheat Muffins

Yield: 12 muffins

These spicy gems are puffy and delicious.

Preheat the oven to 350°F.

1 Tbsp brown sugar
3 Tbsp canola oil
4 Tbsp liquid sweetener
2 Tbsp molasses
1 cup soy yogurt
1 Tbsp grated gingerroot

In a medium mixing bowl, combine the brown sugar, oil, liquid sweetener, molasses, yogurt, and gingerroot.

Dry Ingredients:
1½ cups unbleached white flour
1 cup buckwheat flour
½ tsp cinnamon
¼ tsp ground cloves
1½ tsp baking soda
½ tsp salt

Sift the dry ingredients into the liquid ingredients, and mix well. Spoon the batter into lightly oiled muffin tins, and bake for 15 minutes.

Test to see if the muffins are done by inserting a toothpick in the middle of a muffin. If the toothpick comes out clean, the muffins are done.

Per muffin: Calories: 154, Protein: 3 gm., Fat: 3 gm., Carbohydrates: 27 gm.

Tabouli Muffins

Yield: 12 muffins

Strange but true, these green muffins taste like the famous Middle Eastern dish.

Preheat the oven to 350°F.

½ cup chopped fresh mint
½ cup chopped green onions
¼ cup chopped fresh parsley
2 cloves garlic, chopped
¼ cup lemon juice
2 Tbsp olive oil
2 Tbsp liquid sweetener
2 Tbsp soy sauce
1 cup water

In a blender, combine the mint, green onions, parsley, garlic, lemon juice, oil, liquid sweetener, soy sauce, and water, and pour into a mixing bowl.

1 cup cooked bulgur

Add the bulgur and mix well.

3 cups unbleached white flour
1 tsp baking powder
1 tsp baking soda

Sift the flour, baking powder, and baking soda into the bowl of blended liquid and bulgur. Mix well and spoon into muffin tins. These muffins are large, so you need to fill the cups nearly full. Bake for 18 minutes.

Test to see if the muffins are done by inserting a toothpick in the middle of a muffin. If the toothpick comes out clean, the muffins are done.

Per muffin: Calories: 154, Protein: 4 gm., Fat: 2 gm., Carbohydrates: 29 gm.

Tomato Herb Muffins

Yield: 12 muffins

These are large, bright orange muffins. Delicious with End-of-the-Season Garden Soup (page 26).

Preheat the oven to 350°F.

2½ cups tomato purée (4 medium tomatoes, blended)
1 cup rolled oats
1 tsp crushed rosemary
½ tsp thyme

In a mixing bowl, stir the tomato purée, rolled oats, rosemary, and thyme, and let set for 10 minutes to soften the rolled oats and herbs.

3 Tbsp canola oil
3 Tbsp sorghum molasses

Add the oil and molasses to the bowl of tomato ingredients.

2 cups unbleached white flour
1 cup cornmeal
3 tsp baking powder
½ tsp salt

Sift the flour, cornmeal, baking powder, and salt into the liquid ingredients, and mix. Fill lightly oiled muffin tins to the top, and bake for 20 minutes.

Test to see if the muffins are done by inserting a toothpick in the middle of a muffin. If the toothpick comes out clean, the muffins are done.

Per muffin: Calories: 205, Protein: 5 gm., Fat: 3 gm., Carbohydrates:37 gm.

Accompaniments

Bagels

Yield: 12 bagels

Bagels are easy and fun to make. These bagels are chewy and lend themselves to various accompaniments. A combination of sliced tofu, avocado, pesto, and sprouts are our favorite, but fruit jams and creamy spreads are good too.

2 cups lukewarm water
2 Tbsp liquid sweetener
2 tsp active dry yeast
1½ cups unbleached white flour

In a medium mixing bowl, combine the lukewarm water, liquid sweetener, yeast, and 1½ cups unbleached flour to form a sponge which will bubble up. Let set undisturbed for 10-15 minutes. While the sponge is forming, fill a pot which is at least 9 inches wide with 3-4 quarts of water to a depth of 3½-4 inches, and bring to a boil. Preheat the oven to 350°F.

½ tsp salt
2 Tbsp soy flour
⅓ cup instant gluten flour (vital wheat gluten)
1-1½ cups whole wheat flour
1-1½ cups unbleached white flour

sesame seeds, for topping (optional)
poppy seeds, for topping (optional)

Add the salt, soy flour, gluten flour, whole wheat flour, and remaining white flour to the sponge mixture after it has gotten foamy. Mix well with a wooden spoon, then turn onto a lightly floured counter, and knead for 5-10 minutes. The dough will become smooth and satiny. Only add more flour if it is sticking to your hands. The dough should be soft, not stiff.

Divide the dough into 12 balls. To form the bagels, take each ball and roll it firmly on the counter, pressing down and using the palm of your hand to make a smooth ball. Pick up the ball, press your thumb through the center, and stretch the dough out from the center all around to form a bagel shape. The hole should be about 1 inch across. Set each bagel on a lightly floured surface, and make the next one. Let the bagels set for 10-15 minutes to rise. Lightly sprinkle a baking sheet with cornmeal or oil.

Drop each bagel, in the order that you made them, into a pot of boiling water. Cook 4 at once. Cook for 2½ minutes on one side, then turn over with a slotted spoon, and cook 2½ minutes on the other side. With the slotted spoon, remove a bagel, and place it on the prepared baking sheet with the top side up. Sometimes the bagels turn over during boiling so the flat bottom side (which is sometimes cracked) ends up on top after you've turned them over. Be sure to put that side down on the baking sheet. If you would like to sprinkle the tops with sesame seeds or poppy seeds, do this right after they are removed from the boiling water.

Boil a second batch and put 2 bagels on the first baking sheet. You will have 1 sheet of 6 bagels ready to bake, and 2 more bagels on the next sheet waiting for the next 4 bagels to boil.

Start baking the first batch as soon as the first 6 are boiled; don't wait for the next batch to finish boiling. Bake for 20 minutes. You may need to turn the sheet around in the oven half way through baking if your oven doesn't bake evenly. When the bagels are done, remove from the sheets, place in a large bowl, and cover with a clean dish cloth to keep the bagels soft.

Per bagel: Calories: 177, Protein: 8 gm., Fat: 0 gm., Carbohydrates: 34 gm.

Pumpernickel Bagels

Yield: 12 bagels

2 cups lukewarm water
2 Tbsp liquid sweetener
1 Tbsp blackstrap molasses
2 tsp active dry yeast
1½ cups unbleached white flour

In a medium mixing bowl, combine the warm water, liquid sweetener, blackstrap molasses, yeast, and flour to form a sponge which will bubble up. Let set undisturbed for 15 minutes. While the sponge is forming, fill a pot which is at least 9 inches wide with 3-4 quarts of water to a depth of 3½-4 inches, and bring to a boil. Preheat the oven to 350°F.

½ tsp salt
1 Tbsp carob powder
2 Tbsp cornmeal
½ cup buckwheat flour
1 cup rye flour
1 cup whole wheat flour
1 cup unbleached white flour

Add the remaining ingredients to the sponge mixture, and mix well with a wooden spoon. Follow the directions for making bagels from page 110.

Per bagel: Calories: 182, Protein: 5 gm., Fat: 0 gm., Carbohydrates: 38 gm.

Barb's Apple Biscuits or Loaf

Yield: 12-14 pieces or slices

This bread can be made quickly as a long loaf or, if you have more time, as individual biscuits. This is good with Butternut Soup (page 40).

Dry Ingredients:
2 cups unbleached white flour
½ cup whole wheat flour
3 Tbsp sucanat
2 tsp baking powder
½ tsp salt

3 Tbsp oil
¾ cup nondairy milk

Filling:
3 cups peeled, chopped apples
Juice of 2 lemons (3-4 Tbsp)
⅓ cup brown sugar
½ tsp cinnamon

Preheat the oven to 375°F.

In a medium mixing bowl, mix the dry ingredients until well blended.

Add the oil and nondairy milk, and mix until a stiff, workable dough is formed. Do not knead.

Mix the apples, lemon juice, brown sugar, and cinnamon.

To make the loaf, roll the dough out into a 12 x 18-inch rectangle. Place on a cookie sheet, and spoon the apple filling down the center of the rectangle, the long way. Fold one side and then the other up and over the filling, and pinch to seal at the ends and on top. Bake for 20 minutes. Cool and cut into slices.

To make the filled biscuits, break the dough into 12-14 pieces. Roll out each piece into a 5 to 6-inch circle. Scoop ¼ cup apple filling onto each piece. Draw the dough up over the filling, and pinch together at the top center. Place on a cookie sheet, and bake for 20 minutes.

Per slice: Calories: 152, Protein: 3 gm., Fat: 3 gm., Carbohydrates: 25 gm.

Breadsticks

Yield: 20 breadsticks

Start these before you make your soup. They'll be ready to eat by the time your soup is done. They're good toasted the next day if you have leftovers.

1 Tbsp blackstrap molasses
2 Tbsp liquid sweetener
2 cups lukewarm water
1 package active dry yeast (1½ tsp)
2 cups unbleached white flour

Whisk the molasses, liquid sweetener, water, yeast, and flour in a mixing bowl, and let rise for 10 minutes to form a sponge.

1 Tbsp canola oil
⅓ cup barley flour
2 Tbsp soy flour
1½-2 cups unbleached white flour
1½ cups wheat flour
½ tsp salt

Add the oil, flours, and salt to the rising sponge. Add more flour if the dough is too sticky to work with. Knead for 5-10 minutes until your dough is satiny and soft. Drizzle some oil over the bottom and sides of a bowl, and place the dough back into the bowl. Let rise for 45 minutes.

Divide into 20 walnut-sized balls. Roll out into ½-inch pencil-sized sticks. Place onto 2 cookie sheets with space in between each stick. Preheat the oven to 350°F. Let rise for 15 minutes, and bake for 15 minutes until golden brown.

Per breadstick: Calories: 130, Protein: 4 gm., Fat: 2 gm., Carbohydrates: 25 gm.

Crackers

Yield: One 11 x 17-inch cookie sheet; 40 (2-inch) squares

Crispy crackers are a good addition to any soup. Great for dunking.

Preheat the oven to 375°F.

2 cups unbleached white flour
½ cup nutritional yeast
1 Tbsp sesame seeds
1 tsp garlic powder
1 tsp chili powder
½ tsp salt

Mix the flour, nutritional yeast, sesame seeds, garlic, chili powder, and salt in a mixing bowl.

⅔ cup water
3 Tbsp soy sauce
3 Tbsp oil

Make a hole in the center of the dry ingredients, add the water, soy sauce, and oil, and stir well. You should have a stiff, but workable, dough. Add more water if the dough is too stiff. Press into a cookie sheet, working out from the center, until the dough is evenly covering the whole sheet. You can use a rolling pin to help in this process if you want. Pat down so the top is smooth, and cut into 2-inch square pieces. Poke a fork in the center of each cracker to prevent it from bubbling up. Bake for 15 minutes, or until golden brown. These crackers will be soft when warm but will get crispy as they cool down.

Per 3 crackers: Calories: 36, Protein: 2 gm., Fat: 1 gm., Carbohydrates: 5 gm.

Oat Crackers

Yield: 48 crackers

Preheat the oven to 375°F.

1 cup boiling water
2 cups rolled oats
2 Tbsp sesame seeds

Pour the water over the oats and sesame seeds, and let stand while you're mixing the other ingredients.

½ cup oat flour
½ cup barley flour
1 Tbsp granulated sweetener
½ tsp salt
2 Tbsp canola oil
3 Tbsp soymilk

Add the softened oats to the other ingredients, and mix well. You may want to use your hands for the final mix. Place the dough in the center of a 11 x 17-inch cookie sheet. Press the dough out to the edges, keeping it a uniform thickness all over the pan.

Cut into 48 crackers and bake for 20-25 minutes, until the crackers begin to brown. They will crisp up after they are cool.

Per 3 crackers: Calories: 89, Protein: 3 gm., Fat: 2 gm., Carbohydrates: 12 gm.

Dabo Kola

Yield: 3½ cups

These crunchy, spicy African tidbits are good to nibble on plain or to use as a garnish for soup.

Dry Ingredients:
1 cup white flour
1 cup whole wheat flour
1 Tbsp granulated sweetener
1 tsp paprika
½ tsp salt
½ tsp allspice
½ tsp cinnamon
½ tsp cardamom
½ tsp black pepper
½ tsp ginger
¼ tsp nutmeg
⅛ tsp cayenne

3 Tbsp. canola oil
⅔ cups water

In a medium mixing bowl, mix the dry ingredients.

Add the oil and water to the dry ingredients, and mix well. Turn out onto a lightly floured counter, and knead with your hands until the dough is well mixed.

Break the dough into 4 pieces. Roll each piece out into skinny, round snakes, ¼ inch thick. With a clean pair of kitchen shears, cut off ½-inch nuggets, and place them on a cookie sheet to bake. The nuggets should fill 2 cookie sheets.

Bake for 15-20 minutes, stirring several times so all sides become light brown. They will be crunchy when they cool down. Store in an airtight container if you don't eat them all when they are made.

Per 2 Tbsp.: Calories: 42, Protein: 1 gm., Fat: 1 gm., Carbohydrates: 6 gm.

Herbed Focaccia

Yield: 2 (11-inch) focaccia (12 pieces each)

This round, flat bread lends itself to various toppings. It's quick to make, so you'll have it done in the time it takes for your soup to cook.

2 cups lukewarm water
2 Tbsp liquid granulated sweetener
2 tsp active dry yeast
2 cups unbleached white flour

In a medium mixing bowl, make a sponge of the water, liquid sweetener, yeast, and flour by mixing them together and letting them set until bubbly, about 10 minutes.

1 tsp salt
2 cups whole wheat flour
1 cup unbleached white flour

Add the salt and flours to the bowl, and stir with a spoon until the dough is stiff enough to place on a lightly floured counter. Knead until smooth and satiny. Divide the dough into 2 pieces, and press each piece into a circle about ½ inch thick and 11 inches in diameter. Place on a cookie sheet that has been sprinkled with cornmeal to prevent sticking.

2 Tbsp olive oil
3 Tbsp crushed garlic
2 tsp crushed rosemary
1 tsp dried basil

Spread 1 Tbsp olive oil over the top of each round bread with your fingers. Mix the garlic, rosemary, and basil together with a fork, and sprinkle over the entire top of the breads. Preheat the oven to 350°F. Let the focaccia rise for 10-15 minutes while the oven is preheating. Bake for 20 minutes until the focaccia is golden brown on the bottom and still soft in the center. Cut into wedges and serve warm.

Per wedge: Calories: 99, Protein: 3 gm., Fat: 1 gm., Carbohydrates: 18 gm.

Melina's Herbed Biscuits

Yield: 15 biscuits

These quick biscuits are flavored with dried herbs that make them a taste treat to accompany any soup. I also crumble leftover biscuits up into my tossed salad like croutons.

Preheat the oven to 375°F.

1 cup chopped onions and green peppers
1 Tbsp water

In a medium skillet, steam-fry the onions and green peppers in the 1 Tbsp water. Stir and cook until soft.

Dry Ingredients:
1 cup unbleached white flour
1 cup whole wheat flour
½ cup cornmeal
2 Tbsp nutritional yeast
2 Tbsp granulated sweetener
½ tsp sage
½ tsp basil
½ tsp thyme
1 Tbsp baking powder
½ tsp salt

In a medium bowl, mix the dry ingredients.

3 Tbsp flax seed mixture (page 123)
3 Tbsp canola oil

Add the flax seed mixture, oil, and cooked onion and pepper to the dry ingredients, and mix well.

¾ cup potato water or water

Add the potato water to the bowl, and mix until all water has been absorbed. Take the dough out of the bowl, and place on a lightly floured counter. Press out the dough with the palm of your hands. You may need to flour the top of the dough to prevent your hands from sticking.

Roll or press out ½ inch thick, and cut out biscuits using a 2¾-inch biscuit cutter. Place onto a cookie sheet, slightly touching, and bake for 15 minutes.

Per biscuit: Calories: 111, Protein: 3 gm., Fat: 3 gm., Carbohydrates: 16 gm.

Potato Buns

Yield: 20 (2-inch) round buns

These soft, chewy buns are great for dipping into soup or serving as a bun for a sandwich. This is an easy recipe to divide in half if you don't want to make a full tray of buns, but they freeze well if you do.

2 cups mashed potatoes

2 cups lukewarm potato water

3 Tbsp liquid sweetener

1 Tbsp active dry yeast

1½ cups unbleached white flour

3 Tbsp canola oil

1 tsp salt

⅓ cup instant gluten flour (vital wheat flakes)

3 cups whole wheat flour

3½ cups unbleached white flour

Combine the mashed potatoes, potato water, liquid sweetener, yeast, and flour in a medium mixing bowl. Let set for 10 minutes until a bubbly sponge forms.

Add the oil, salt, and flours to the liquid ingredients, and mix well. Turn out onto a lightly oiled surface, and knead until soft and satiny. Oil the edges of the mixing bowl, and put the dough back in it to rise until doubled.

Punch the dough down and form into 20 balls. Place them evenly spaced on a large cookie tray, not touching. They will rise into each other to form soft buns. Preheat the oven to 350°F. Let the buns rise for 15 minutes while the oven is preheating. Bake for 20-25 minutes. Cover with a towel upon removing from the oven if you like a soft crust.

Per bun: Calories: 211, Protein: 7 gm., Fat: 2 gm., Carbohydrates: 39 gm.

Scones

Yield: 12 scones

Irish raisin biscuits are fun to make and good with soup.

Preheat the oven to 375°F.

Dry Ingredients:
1½ cups white flour
½ cup whole wheat flour
1½ Tbsp granulated sweetener
2 tsp baking powder
½ tsp salt

In a medium mixing bowl, combine the dry ingredients.

3 Tbsp flax seed mixture (page 123)
3 Tbsp canola oil

Mix the flax seed mixture and oil into the bowl of dry ingredients. Mix with a fork until well blended.

7 Tbsp soy yogurt
½ cup raisins

Add the soy yogurt and raisins, and mix until all the liquid is absorbed. Don't over mix. Flatten the dough onto a lightly floured counter. With your hands, press the dough out into a ½-inch thick square or rectangle. With a blunt knife, cut into triangles and place on a cookie sheet. Bake for 13 minutes. These are best if served warm.

Per scone: Calories: 123, Protein: 3 gm., Fat: 3 gm., Carbohydrates: 19 gm.

Sesame Sticks

Yield: 24 sticks

Preheat the oven to 350°F.

Dry Ingredients:
1 cup unbleached white flour
2 Tbsp barley flour
1 Tbsp granulated sweetener
½ tsp salt
½ tsp baking powder

Stir together the dry ingredients in a small mixing bowl.

2 Tbsp canola oil
½ cup nondairy milk

Add the oil and nondairy milk to the bowl of dry ingredients, and mix well. You can use your hands for the final mixing to make sure all the dry ingredients are blended into the liquid. This is a stiff dough.

5 Tbsp sesame seeds

Divide the dough into 12 pieces. Roll out each piece into a stick 6-7 inches long and ⅜-½ inch wide. Narrow sticks will be crispier. Cut each stick in half, and roll in a shallow bowl of sesame seeds. Press the sticks firmly into the seeds so they become imbedded in the dough. Place on an ungreased cookie sheet, not touching each other. Bake for 25 minutes until golden brown. Let cool and enjoy with a tasty soup. The sesame seeds will fall off if they are moved around a lot, but you can gather up the loose seeds and use them for garnish on your soup.

Per stick: Calories: 43, Protein: 1 gm., Fat: 2 gm., Carbohydrates: 5 gm.

Glossary

Amaranth Flour: Flour made from a tiny, round grain that is about 16% protein. Amaranth contains no gluten so it needs to be combined with other flours to make baked goods that will rise properly.

Barley Flour: Milled from barley, a grain which is easy to digest. Barley flour is light colored and a tasty addition to baked products.

Barley Malt: A mild liquid sweetener made from barley.

Blackstrap Molasses: A dark cane syrup that contains several B vitamins and minerals and is rich in iron.

Brown Rice Syrup: A thick liquid sweetener with a mild flavor made from brown rice.

Buckwheat Flour: There are two types of buckwheat flour—a dark flour made from roasted buckwheat (kasha) and a lighter flour made from raw buckwheat.

Cane Molasses: Also known as sorghum molasses, cane molasses is made from the crushed stalks of the sorghum plant. It is good over pancakes and waffles as well as in baked goods.

Couscous: A quick-cooking grain made from cracked semolina wheat.

Flax Seeds: A good source of omega-3 essential fatty acids. To make egg replacer from flax seeds, blend up ½ cup flax seeds with 2 cups warm water. The seeds will remain partially intact but will be evenly distributed in the water. Store in the refrigerator for up to 2 weeks. Use this mixture as an egg substitute in pancakes, muffins, breads, cakes, biscuits etc.

Instant Gluten Flour (Vital Wheat Gluten): Wheat flour which has had the starch and bran removed, leaving only the protein portion of the wheat. Not to be confused with "high-gluten bread flour." With gluten flour you can add water and have raw gluten instantly. By simmering in broth, you can have seitan (cooked gluten).

Liquid Aminos: A seasoning made from soybeans. It is dark like soy sauce but is not fermented. Liquid aminos contains 16 amino acids.

Liquid Sweeteners: These can be cane molasses, maple syrup, blackstrap molasses, barley malt, etc.

Maple Syrup: Made from the boiled sap of the sugar maple tree, maple syrup is a rich tasting (and expensive) sweetener.

Millet: A small, round, white grain. Millet develops a good flavor when it is toasted in a dry skillet before it is cooked. When added to soups, it thickens the soup by absorbing liquid. Millet is the only grain that is alkaline (acid-neutralizing) when cooked.

Miso: A salty paste made from soybeans (and sometimes grains) which have been cooked and aged. Miso can be light, medium, or dark in color and can be used as a base for soups, salad dressings, and dips. The enzymes present in miso can aid digestion if they have not been boiled, so add it at the end of cooking.

Molasses: A thick, dark, strong-tasting syrup made from cane sugar.

Nondairy Milk: Milks made from nuts, grains, or beans. There are commercially produced milks made from almonds, cashews, rice, oats, or soybeans.

Nutritional Yeast: An inactive yeast that is high in B vitamins and protein. Nutritional yeast is yellow and has a pleasant, cheesy flavor. It should not to be confused with brewer's yeast, which is bitter, or active dry yeast (baking yeast), which is used to make bread rise. It makes a wonderful condiment, sprinkled over soup.

Oatmeal, Cooked: Make extra oatmeal in the morning for breakfast so you'll have some on hand in the refrigerator for baking. It makes a great egg replacer, adding moisture and binding qualities to your muffin mixes. Use about 2 tablespoons of cooked oatmeal for each egg being replaced.

Quinoa: A high-protein grain. When boiled like rice, quinoa becomes a light, nutty, soft grain. Quinoa must be rinsed with water before it is used to remove a bitter substance from its surface.

Rice Flour: Depending on what variety of rice is ground, rice flour can vary immensely. Sweet rice makes a sticky flour. Brown rice makes a flour that adds crispness to baked goods.

Sorghum: see Cane Molasses

Soy Flour: Made from ground soybeans, this yellow flour makes baked goods brown easily and increases the protein content.

Stevia: Derived from the powered leaf of a South American herb, stevia is a calorie-free sweetener that can be substituted for sugar.

Sucanat: Dehydrated sugar cane juice that retains all the naturally occurring vitamins, minerals, and trace elements. You can use it to replace white sugar, but it is expensive.

Tahini: A smooth paste made by grinding roasted or raw sesame seeds.

Tempeh: Tempeh is made from soybeans (and sometimes grains) which have been steamed, then inoculated with mushroom-like spores and fermented. It is high in protein and can be sliced, grated, or cubed to make many delicious dishes.

Tofu: Tofu (or soybean curd) is made by solidifying soymilk with a coagulant and straining off the liquid, then pressing the curds into a block. Tofu can be regular (very solid) or silken (smooth) and either soft, firm, or extra-firm in density. It is now available in non-fat/low-fat varieties, as well as full-fat.

Textured Vegetable Protein: Made from extruded, defatted soy flour which has been cooked under pressure. It is dry and must be rehydrated. Textured vegetable protein can be used as a quick-to-cook replacement for ground beef. You can order it from The Mail Order Catalog P.O. Box 180, Summertown, TN 38483 (800-695-2241).

Unbleached White Flour: Wheat flour which has had the bran and germ removed but has not been bleached.

Index

Ask your store to carry these books, or you may order directly from:

The Book Publishing Company   *Or call: 1-800-695-2241*
P.O. Box 99   *Please add $2.50 per book*
Summertown, TN 38483   *for shipping*

20 Minutes to Dinner.....................$12.95
Almost No-Fat Cookbook...................12.95
Almost No-Fat Holiday....................12.95
Becoming Vegetarian......................15.95
Burgers 'N Fries 'N Cinnamon Buns.........6.95
Cooking Healthy w/One Foot Out the Door...8.95
Delicious Jamaica........................11.95
Fabulous Beans *by Barb Bloomfield*.......9.95
Flavors of India.........................12.95
From a Traditional Greek Kitchen.........12.95
From the Tables of Lebanon...............12.95
Good Time Eatin' in Cajun Country.........9.95
Health Promoting Cookbook................12.95
Indian Cooking At Your House.............12.95
Lighten Up w/Louise Hagler...............11.95
Natural Lunchbox.........................12.95
New Farm Vegetarian Cookbook..............8.95
Now and Zen Epicure......................17.95
Nutritional Yeast.........................9.95
Olive Oil Cookery........................10.95
Shiitake Way..............................9.95
Shoshoni Cookbook........................12.95
Solar Cooking.............................8.95
Soyfoods Cookery..........................9.95
Sprout Garden.............................8.95
Table for Two............................12.95
Taste of Mexico..........................13.95
Tasty Bytes...............................9.95
Tempeh Cookbook..........................10.95
Tofu Cookery.............................15.95
Tofu Quick & Easy.........................8.95
TVP® Cookbook.............................7.95
Uncheese Cookbook........................11.95
Uprisings................................13.95
Vegan Vittles............................11.95